Music Therapy in Children's Hospices

also by Mercédès Pavlicevic

Community Music Therapy
Mercédès Pavlicevic and Gary Ansdell
Foreword by Even Ruud
ISBN 978 1 84310 124 6

Groups in Music
Strategies from Music Therapy
Mercédès Pavlicevic
ISBN 978 1 84310 081 2

Music Therapy: Intimate Notes
Mercédès Pavlicevic
ISBN 978 1 85302 692 8

Music Therapy in Context
Music, Meaning and Relationship
Mercédès Pavlicevic
Preface by Colwyn Trevarthen
ISBN 978 1 85302 434 4

of related interest

Music Therapy in Palliative Care
New Voices
Edited by David Aldridge
ISBN 978 1 85302 739 0

Journeys into Palliative Care
Roots and Reflections
Edited by Christina Mason
ISBN 978 1 84310 030 0

Being Mindful, Easing Suffering
Reflections on Palliative Care
Christopher Johns
ISBN 978 1 84310 212 0

Filling a Need While Making Some Noise
A Music Therapist's Guide to Pediatrics
Kathy Irvine Lorenzato
Foreword by Kay Roskam
ISBN 978 1 84310 819 1

Music Therapy in Children's Hospices
Jessie's Fund in Action

Edited by Mercédès Pavlicevic

Foreword by Victoria Wood

Jessica Kingsley Publishers
London and Philadelphia

'Morning Song' on p.37 from *Collected Poems* by Christy Brown published by Secker & Warburg.
Reproduced by permission of The Random House Group Limited.

First published in 2005
by Jessica Kingsley Publishers
116 Pentonville Road
London N1 9JB, UK
and
400 Market Street, Suite 400
Philadelphia, PA 19106, USA

www.jkp.com

Library of Congress Cataloging in Publication Data
Music therapy in children's hospices : celebrating Jessie's Fund / edited by Mercedes Pavlicevic;
foreword by Victoria Wood.
     p. cm.
Includes bibliographical references and index.
ISBN-10: 1-84310-254-4 (pbk.)
ISBN-13: 978-1-84310-254-0 (pbk.)
1. Music therapy. 2. Children--Hospice care. I. Pavlicevic, Mercedes. II. Wood, Victoria, 1953–
ML3920.M8978 2005
615.8' 5154--dc22

                                                                        2004025502

British Library Cataloguing in Publication Data
A CIP catalogue record for this book is available from the British Library

ISBN 978 1 84310 254 0

Printed and Bound in Great Britain by
Athenaeum Press, Gateshead, Tyne and Wear

Dedicated to Jessie, and to children like her everywhere, who have brought joy, sorrow and strength to those who love them

Contents

ACKNOWLEDGEMENTS   9

Foreword   11
Victoria Wood

Introduction   15
Mercédès Pavlicevic

1 **'When I grow up…'**   21
   Lesley Schatzberger

2 **The beginnings of music therapy in our hospice**   37
   Cathy Ibberson

3 **Music and medicine: Music therapy within a medical setting**   48
   Catherine Sweeney-Brown

4 **A creative response to loss: Developing a music therapy
   group for bereaved siblings**   62
   Jane Mayhew

5 **Brief encounters**   81
   Ceridwen Rees

6 **'A Bohemian Rhapsody': Using music technology to fulfil
   the aspirations of teenage lads with muscular dystrophy**   95
   Neil Eaves

7 **The open music therapy group session**   110
   Brigitte Schwarting

8 **Living community: Music therapy with children and adults
   in a hospice setting**   124
   Graeme Davis

9 **'This musical life': Tŷ Hafan Children's Hospice –
   a place for living**   139
   Diane Wilkinson

10 From hospice to home: Music therapy outreach   **147**
Kathryn Nall and Elinor Everitt

11 Needing support: A therapist's perspective   **159**
Gill Cubitt

Before we conclude...   **169**
Mercédès Pavlicevic

Conclusion: Working together in music therapy   **170**
Chris Stratton and Jane Mayhew

LIST OF CONTRIBUTORS   178

LIST OF JESSIE'S FUND CD TRACKS   183

SUBJECT INDEX   184

AUTHOR INDEX   188

CD ORDER FORM   189

Acknowledgements

This book would not have been possible without the initiative, inspiration, help and support of various people:

- the music therapists of Jessie's Fund, who courageously put their work under the spotlight, so to speak, and delivered their chapters graciously and punctually
- the children and their families, who generously allowed the material to be used in this book
- Victoria Wood, whose active interest has been enormously important
- Neil Eaves, who expertly transformed the informally recorded tracks into a CD available alongside this book
- Erich Kadow, who understood the spirit of our work and designed the cover
- Mikaela Griffiths, whose patience and pernicketiness ensured that this editor's scribbles were neatly typed in
- Sandra Patruno, of Jessica Kingsley Publishers, for her professionalism and prompt replies to endless queries
- the supporters of Jessie's Fund, whose financial input has made possible the work you read about in these pages
- the Madeline Mabey Trust and the Scarfe Charitable Trust, for funding the editorial costs
- Lesley Schatzberger, for being the driving force, the mailbox and the epitome of patience and stability through all this
- Mercédès Pavlicevic, for believing in the idea of writing this book in the first place, and without whose experience, guidance and encouragement the chapters making up the whole would never have come together as a unified work
- Jessie, whose life and its ending gave us a beginning...

Lesley Schatzberger, York, UK
Mercédès Pavlicevic, Pretoria, South Africa
August 2004

Foreword

When I was first pregnant in 1988, and mooching round bookshops looking for useful information ('How to breastfeed while writing sitcoms' unfortunately seems still to be unavailable), one of my purchases was a book called something like *The Working Mother's Handbook*. It was hugely encouraging, and one of the mothers quoted was a Lesley Schatzberger, musician, mother of two, York. It was a name I had come across before, a school friend who played the clarinet. I wondered idly if it was her, had my baby, was too busy to read *The Working Mother's Handbook*, wedged open the bathroom window with it, and got on with being a comedian.

A long long time later, I had a letter from Lesley, asking me to be a patron of her charity Jessie's Fund. I was so sad to realise that one of the two children mentioned in that book, one of those little daughters of that working musician in York, had died, and this was a charity set up in her name.

Well of course there are personal tragedies driving the setting up of any charity, but there were other reasons why I felt able to come on board. Partly my old bond with Lesley, but mainly my feeling about music – that it is a much more subtle and expressive means of communication than written or spoken language. I was also very taken with the core idea of the hospice as a place where life is lived fully up to the moment of death, that those last few months, weeks or days can be a time of creativity and exploration.

★

The first tune I ever played was 'Polly Wolly Doodle', top speed on our piano with one finger, more likely to drive someone into a hospice than help them while they're in it. My father had written the names of the notes on the keys and under the dots on the music and I was off. I whipped through that dreary old songbook, 'Last Rose of Summer', 'British Grenadiers' (yes, there should be more singing in schools, but please, not that) – I loved all those tunes, even Bobby Shaftoe and his awful trousers.

I carried on for some years, happily bashing my way through the piles of moth-eaten music my mother bought from sale rooms (she was a compulsive bargain seeker; we had a hall crammed with bags of shoe lasts and the costumes from *No No Nanette*).

Then I went to grammar school, in Bury (not the St Edmunds one, the black pudding one). Music turned from a private pleasure to a public activity fraught with tension. Picture, if you can bear it, 35 navy-jumpered lumps plodding through *Eine Kleine Nachtmusik* on recorders. Music lovers from as far afield as Whitefield were chucking rocks through the windows and throwing themselves under racehorses.

We were offered the chance to burn our recorders and learn another instrument. My mother moved aside the eight dining chairs she'd bought for a fiver and found me a trumpet. For some reason she was reluctant to buy me a proper case, and made me one out of a blue plastic tablecloth. If she hadn't lost my post office book I'd have left home.

Then we formed a school orchestra. It was a strange line-up, two percussion, two brass, loads of flutes and clarinets because they were easy to take on the bus, and a couple of violins that sounded like they'd come out of a cracker. We were all terrible and the music mistress who conducted was no André Previn. She was more like Morecambe and Wise. Every piece had to be taken at the pace of the worst player (we were a grammar school but our orchestra was comprehensive). Handel's *Water Music* was like a leak dripping into a bucket – thank heavens we never did the 'Minute Waltz', we'd have all missed our last bus home. Whenever I hear something from our school repertoire played properly on the radio, I fan myself and go, 'Crikey, they're taking that at a lick.'

As Lesley says in the book, we were both misfits at school. I know I was a terrible uncooked mixture of shyness, lumpiness, rage, fat, spots, talent, idleness, ambition, but the first day I sat in the middle of the trumpet section of Bury Military Band, and heard professional-level musicians soar their way through 'Pineapple Poll', a little door in my heart opened up and I knew that the music was feeding my soul and my spirit and that I was more than a lumpy old adolescent.

★

I feel privileged to be a part of Jessie's Fund, however small. I have huge respect for the way Lesley has turned a devastating personal loss into something that will benefit so many people in the same situation. I'm glad to be connected with a charity whose aims I can really understand and support. And I feel I'm beginning to learn a little about living in the moment, about taking the emphasis off the future, with its imaginary achievements and goals, and just having life as it is, now.

That's not to say I'm abandoning my plan of a world-dominating recorder group...

Victoria Wood, London, UK

Introduction

Mercédès Pavlicevic

Music *is* life, and like it, is inextinguishable.

Carl Nielsen, Symphony No. 4, 'The Inextinguishable'

Working on this book has kept me returning to a question I once heard at a music therapy presentation. The question went something like: *why does a child about to die also want to sing?*[1] It is a simple and profound question: how many of us, when we feel low in energy or mildly unwell, feel like singing? Which prompts another question – can we sing when we're not quite up to it? These children do. With energy and vitality that is large as life. Yet many of them are about to die. Some are terminally, desperately ill; some are suddenly, brutally catapulted towards illness and death; others seem to be interminably ill – and exhausted by their illness; others, still very much alive, know that their brother or sister will not be so for very much longer. In this book, children continue, each of them, to make music, to smile at the sound of a chime bar, to move their foot when nothing else moves any longer or to dance about, brandishing beaters and ordering the music therapist to shape up – the music needs *more*! More life! More vitality! More energy! NOW! And they are watched by incredulous parents and care staff, whose lasting memories may well

---

1   Thanks to Gary Ansdell for permission to adapt this question.

become this music of life that their child insisted on breathing and creating, even in the last moments of living.

But let's begin with music. What does it mean, how does it manage to get under our skin, apparently throughout our lives; why do we love it so, why does it drive us mad when it is too loud, when it sounds too strange or too 'modern' and not like the music *we* used to know back in those days; why do we feel some sense of embarrassment when we're made to voice those dreadful words, 'I'm not musical – at school I had to leave the choir – I can't hold a tune'? Our response to this, as music therapists, is: 'Whose tune are you wanting to hold? To whose tune do you want to sing?'

What you will read in this book are stories of children singing and playing music in their own way. They are facilitated by music therapists whose special skill is to invite and support the children's breathing, their movements, the qualities of their stillness or restlessness, their vocal sounds and their music-making, no matter how unconventional or idio-syncratic, and no matter how minute. Music therapists know how to listen and to create moments of great intimacy, beauty and magic, with music. At the end of this book, Chris says this about his time with music therapist Jane Mayhew: 'We also have a bloody good "laugh". We under-stand one another. When I say "grey", normally someone assumes either "black" or "white"; not Jane, she…thinks "grey".'

One of the deliciously intimate things about music therapy is the feeling of being heard. Whatever and however you do your music, the music therapist listens and, together with you, makes it into something of great significance and beauty. Into something utterly alive: in Chapter 3, Mark struggles to eat, is intensely nauseous and dizzy because of his brain tumour; he is expected to live for a few days at the most. Hours later he is engrossed in playing the drum and cymbal, with an alert energy that Catherine Sweeney-Brown reflects in her piano improvisation with him. After 40 minutes of lively playing he smiles at her and says, 'That was pretty good, let's do another one.' Catherine is concerned that he might wear himself out, and Mark insists on continuing. In Chapter 7, Brigitte Schwarting manages to be available to each member of the group – almost miraculously, she 'tunes in' to Emily, who 'smiles but hardly ever responds'; Charlotte, who 'predictably responds by vocalising on the note "D"'; Leo, who throws away the beaters he has been handed to play; Susie, the new staff member who seems unsure as to what is going on; and Arnold, who arrives from school, throws his bag on the floor and asks Brigitte for the guitar. Multi-tasking, multi-tuning, multi-focus, within a single song. In Chapter 5, Ceridwen Rees poignantly describes a moment in music therapy when Harry, all of 20 months old, smiles, in the arms of his mother. Harry will die two days later. Some months pass, and Ceridwen meets Harry's mum, Sam, who says to her, 'That was one good moment – the absolute extreme opposite of the horrendous memory of his last breaths. If I didn't have that good and precious moment…I don't know how I'd cope.'

How do the music therapists themselves cope? This is one of the undertows of this book, and there are clues here and there of the astonishing frankness and vulnerability of dedicated professionals: Ceridwen dreads working with Harry – what can she possibly offer him in one session, when he is so very ill? Neil Eaves, in Chapter 6, is put on the spot by Imran, who wants to know what's happening in the 'quiet room'; Neil knows that this is the moment of truth: 'I knew I had to be honest,' he writes, candidly. 'I asked Imran if he had heard of the quiet room, and when he nodded, I said that there was somebody in there.' Someone has died, and at 18 Imran, who is acutely aware of his prognosis, takes it on the chin. Imran copes, and helps Neil to cope too. It is a turning moment in their relationship. In Chapter 8, Graeme Davis invites us to accompany him through a day in music therapy. Within hours of one another, he accompanies Mary's energetic and deliberate beating and singing with an upbeat bluesy style that invites the two staff members to join in and become the 'backing band'; he conducts a relaxation group session, choosing music to enable the adults gradually to release their stresses and tensions; he works quietly with little Lucy, whose response is to open her eyes while he sings; and he plays Bach and Chopin in the room where Mr Jones is dying and Mrs Jones holds her husband's hand. All in a day's work. In Chapter 9, Diane Wilkinson speaks of preparing music for the Christmas concert, for services of Thanksgiving and Remembrance; while Ceridwen Rees describes having to put aside her own grief at the loss of Alex, to acquiesce in his sister Jessica's request for help to sing at her brother's service. Some months later, Jessica says to Ceridwen, 'This song[2] gave me the chance to do something for Alex', while their mother says, 'Some memories fade but this will always remain clear…a very special reminder to her of her brother.' In Chapter 10, Kathryn Nall and Elinor Everitt describe the ongoing decisions, preparations and evaluations necessary to secure funding for extending music therapy from the hospice into children's homes; while in Chapter 4, Jane Mayhew's description and reflection of work with a group of bereaved siblings gives us an inkling of the innovative nature of this work – setting up a new group, doing new things, with children who have lost their brother or sister and are enormously courageous in their vulnerabilities and uncertainties. In a sense they show the music therapist what to do next, and because she is highly skilled in listening to them, their music and their unspoken needs, she responds accordingly. In Chapter 11, Gill Cubitt invites us to accompany Viola Truenote, newly qualified, as she begins her work in a children's hospice, is faced with death in a tangible way and realises the importance of a supportive, collegial network, as provided by meetings with other music therapists who work in hospices.

Which brings us to the beginning, and to Jessie's Fund. It seems incredible, reading this book, that some ten years ago there was no music therapy provision for children in hospices. The description of Lesley Schatzberger and Cathy Ibberson, motoring to Bristol to meet with music therapist Leslie Bunt for advice on how best to begin, has a flavour of intrepid travelling; travelling with an idea in mind, an inner pressure to 'do' something; a certainty that this is the way to begin, despite not being quite certain about the unfolding of it. Lesley and her family have recently lost Jessie, while Cathy has just begun working as a music therapist at Martin House, were Jessie died only weeks before. Lesley and Cathy meet, begin talking about music and music therapy, and the rest is what you will read about in this book.

This book (and the Jessie's Fund CD) is a celebration of Jessie's Fund in action – children, parents, staff and therapists singing, dancing, playing, thinking, being put on the spot, grieving, crying quietly and

---

2   This song is on the CD that can be ordered directly from Jessie's Fund, using the order form at the back of this book.

vociferously, choosing music, planning their day, being vitalised, being intimate, being listened to, in, with and through music. This book is also about good work. Work that is focused, flexible and spontaneous; work that is playful, that responds to the moment, that is able to do away with unnecessary bureaucracy and complications; work that reaches the heart of the matter. The heart of the matter is, quite simply, music and life.

Chapter One

'When I grow up...'

Lesley Schatzberger

I want to be a pilot in the sky
In a helicopter risen up very high
I want to be a sailor sailing on the sea
That's my ambition for what I want to be.

I want to be a starfish looking like a star
I want to go and investigate up in space so far
I want to be a shop-keeper behind the massive till
I want to be a pharmacist looking up a pill.

I want to be a musician on my world round trip
I want to be a rabbit, hippity hop hip hip.

Jessica George (9), February 1994

Jessie stood at the threshold of her bedroom in that warm and gentle moment after her evening bath, wearing a long nightdress which would not have looked out of place in the nineteenth century, and asked, 'Mummy, how old do I have to be before I'm in a professional orchestra?' This may seem an unusually focused ambition for a nine-year-old, but music had always played a big part in Jessie's life. The child of two professional musicians, she had not only been exposed to live music-making from her very beginnings, but had also frequently accompanied us on overseas tours with her sister, Hannah. Thus it was that our younger daughter contemplated a life steeped in music. As destiny would have it, there was to be no growing up.

*Jessie, wearing the nightdress mentioned, trying out
a full-size violin still much too large for her, 1992*

Jessica May George was born on 22 October 1984. Hannah was then a
characterful two-year-old, and it was difficult to imagine how our new
daughter would be able to command as much attention as her older sister!
We need not have worried – our daughters were quite different personali-
ties right from the beginning, and it intrigued us to observe how
fledgling character traits which emerged during their early months
formed these two strong, and in many ways complementary, little individuals. Hannah, with her wonderful shock of wild, auburn curls, was
gregarious, effervescent and often fiery. Her extrovert persona belied a
soft centre with more than a touch of vulnerability. Jessica, slighter in
stature, had fair and silky locks, was a little more reserved and tended
towards occasional stubborn sulks in place of her sister's passing erup-
tions. Yet she had an enormous inner strength, which would be tested all
too soon.

Both girls had a great sense of humour and enjoyed playing and
laughing together: Hannah's tinkling peals and Jessica's slightly hoarse
giggles would ring through the house, and when Jessie laughed in her
peculiarly wicked way her father, Alan, called it her 'maniacal cackle'.

Both Alan and Hannah called her Jessie, while I more often used her unabbreviated name. She liked her middle name too, and later included it in her signature. She could be amazingly forthright with people but somehow managed to avoid causing offence, even when saying something which might seem a blistering criticism if uttered by anyone else! Because of our musical connections we lived an extremely sociable life, and our large Victorian town house was frequently full of visiting friends/colleagues with whom we were working at the time, or who were giving concerts in the area. Our children would always engage them – few could manage to resist being drawn into play with them, and towards evening our big kitchen would be bustling with activity as visitors and children played and Alan or I prepared the meal.

Like many children, our daughters had natural artistic flair, and (true to form) expressed it differently. Hannah loved to dance, always moving with grace, and although she took piano, then flute, then singing lessons, music was not her passion. Jessica seemed a string player from the start and learnt the violin and later the piano. I loved to watch the concentration on her face as she worked on her violin; her little mouth mobile without her realising it. (This, like so many of her 'isms', would be echoed years later by Jacob, the little brother she never met.) We looked forward to seeing our daughters blossom into young women. Soon after we passed the milestone of our firstborn making the transition into secondary education, at eleven years of age, our world began to collapse.

Jessie's ninth birthday was memorable because we had arranged to take her to the cinema with her friends as part of the celebrations, but at the last minute the schedule changed and there was no appropriate film. For years we had avoided buying a VCR player, wanting to minimise the amount of time our children spent viewing. Their plaintive pleas to be able to watch videos like all their friends had fallen upon deaf ears, but this was the day before the party, there was no film to see and we had a worried little girl whose birthday was about to be spoilt! So we jumped down from our high horse, rushed out to buy a VCR player and hired *My Girl*. The day was saved. It was memorable for another reason: her ninth was to be Jessica's last birthday.

In mid-November 1993, about three weeks after her birthday, Jessica started to talk about seeing two of everything. She already had spectacles to correct mild astigmatism, but wore them rarely. Wearing them now had no effect on the double vision. We went to see the optician, who checked her eyes and reported that there was no problem; a mild bout of flu had probably weakened her eye muscles temporarily. I was uneasy and I said in as unconcerned a way as possible – to avoid alarming Jessie – that I was aware that an early symptom of a brain tumour could be double vision, so I was pleased to hear that she felt there was nothing to be concerned about. She made reassuring noises and we left. I did not feel at all reassured but Jessie, in the innocence of childhood which was to be so helpful in the coming months, trusted her and was perfectly happy. Within a few days she noticed that her balance was sometimes uncertain. At first she found it amusing, and she would twirl around, falling to the floor laughing, get up and do it all over again. Soon she was feeling unmistakably dizzy, and we booked an appointment with the family doctor. He diagnosed labyrinthitis, an infection of the inner ear, pre-scribed a course of antibiotics, and asked us to return a week later. Jessie was rather proud of her exotic-sounding malady, taking delight in telling all her friends about it just to give herself the opportunity to roll the impressive sequence of syllables around her mouth.

As we were having our meal one evening, during the week between the two doctor's appointments, Hannah said, 'Have you ever noticed that Jessie has a bit of a squint?' Characteristically, Jessie thought this was funny, fooling around and joking about it. Both Alan and I were certain that the barely perceptible squint was new: my unease was changing into a sense of foreboding. By the time we went to the doctor the second time, on Monday 6 December 1993, Jessie had become decidedly unsteady on her feet – it was absolutely clear to me that this was no ear infection. The doctor acted quickly, referring us to the paediatrician at the local York hospital, estimating that we would probably be given an appointment within two to three weeks. When the hospital telephoned us the following morning to say that our appointment was to be the next day I felt sure that this swift action signified a serious problem: in my heart I knew, with a mother's intuition, that our little girl had a brain tumour.

On Wednesday 8 December we saw the consultant and Jessica was immediately admitted as an in-patient to the hospital in York. At this stage we were given no clear indication of a possible diagnosis, but it was

Jessie on Hannah's lap, Hannah on Lesley's lap, Lesley on Alan's lap! 1989

evident that there was enormous concern. Early the following morning, after Jessica had been checked by a nurse each and every hour through the night (mercifully sleeping between checks, while I simply shivered the long hours away as I lay by her side), we were transferred the 25 miles to Leeds General Infirmary by ambulance. Here we found ourselves in bewildering surroundings – a world full of children so clearly very sick, examination rooms, radiology departments, endless corridors. No time was lost in settling Jessica into her bed in the corner of the ward, and then in moving her to other rooms for various investigatory procedures. By that afternoon we had our devastating diagnosis: an aggressive tumour in the brain stem which was inoperable. The prognosis was extremely poor, but she was to be given the maximum dosage of radiotherapy. We decided to be open with Jessie and explain exactly what was wrong with her, stopping short of telling her that it was life-threatening. The following morning she woke up well before dawn and wept a few tears, not over her illness, but because she was missing taking part in the school Christmas play that day.

By now, just two days after we had taken the ten-minute walk from our home to the hospital, Jessica could barely walk at all. In her hospital bed, she acted out her role in the school play to me, saying 'and this is the part where I wave'. I was thankful for that innocence.

That evening we returned home and addressed the need to borrow a wheelchair. The circumstances we found ourselves in seemed surreal – how could our lives have changed so dramatically in such a short space of time? Within a week Jessica started on her twice-a-day, 23-day course of radiotherapy, and although she was nauseous much of the time and had difficulty sleeping, she seemed accepting of her situation. I worked hard on absorbing as much of the emotional trauma as possible in order to protect both her and Hannah – who was going through her own confusion and pain, suddenly having to mature far beyond her eleven years.

We had to face the fact that there was little hope of Jessica surviving more than six months, even with all that conventional medical practice could offer. But I was sure that there were other ways in which we could improve her chances, and I became totally focused on researching alternative and complementary treatments. We were already seeing a homeopathic practitioner regularly: she prescribed a number of remedies aimed at helping Jessie to cope with the intense radiation treatment and she made herself available on the phone, at any time of day or night. Not only did the remedies ease Jessie's nausea and minimise the soreness caused by the radiation, but the homeopath's calm and comforting presence was a godsend for me. Late each evening, after the girls were in bed, I would pore over books describing the many alternative approaches to treating cancers, trying to understand the sometimes contradictory information with which I was presented. After some weeks and a number of phone calls to various clinics in the UK and overseas, Alan and I came to the conclusion that the greatest hope lay in a nutritional therapy devised by a physician in New York. His theory was that if the body could be elevated into a super-healthy state, the immune system would do its utmost to suppress the uncontrolled division and multiplication of the tumour cells.

By the beginning of February Jessie was beginning to feel much better. The radiotherapy had shrunk the tumour and she was walking and even attempting the odd half day at school. It was now two months since Alan or I had worked (the itinerant life of a freelance musician could not be contemplated), and we were touched by the generous gifts of money our colleagues sent to compensate for some of our loss of income. More than that, two of our musician friends had set about starting a campaign to raise money for the intended treatment in New York. One of them visited us and told us all about the plan: I remember Jessie's eyes opening wide as she realised that such a large musical community was supporting her. We started to talk about the practical aspects of such a campaign, like opening a separate bank account and giving it a name. After one or two unimaginative suggestions from her parents, Jessie, with her unique, husky giggle, said simply, 'How about calling it Jessie's Fund?'

As Jessie was steadily becoming stronger, we were allowing ourselves to be just the tiniest bit more optimistic about the future. It was at this point that we had a routine appointment with the paediatrician whom we had seen on our very first visit to the hospital in York, before our admission and subsequent transfer to Leeds. He suggested that we might consider visiting Martin House, the children's hospice near Wetherby, Yorkshire. I could feel myself recoil like a snail withdrawing into its shell at the very mention of a children's hospice: this was my period of denial, and I believed we would beat this 'blob', as Jessie called it a few weeks earlier. She had written during her radiotherapy:

> I will fight my bloomin' blob
> I'll fight it away and away
> I will fight it till it's gone
> I'll fight it till the great day

She had also written a little rhyme which we sang to the 'Ode to Joy' tune from Beethoven's Ninth Symphony:

> Day by day I fight my tumour
> I'll kill every rotten cell
> One by one I kill them off
> And I will soon be fit and well

We could almost make ourselves believe that this would become reality during her period of remission, and we were not ready even to imagine needing the services of a children's hospice. After all, wasn't a hospice a grim last post; a place to die?

At the beginning of April Jessie was well enough for us to make concrete plans to take her to New York within weeks. The physician we had arranged to see did not normally treat children because his regimen required the patient to follow a restricted diet and take a large number of supplements in the form of tablets, and he doubted that a child would be able to cope with it. However, Jessie had already been eating as pure a diet as we could provide (organic produce, no additives, very little fat or sugar) and taking 28 tablets of vitamin and mineral supplements a day, so he decided to take her on. We had urged him to do so, because one of our colleagues had been diagnosed with malignant melanoma a few years previously, had been given a poor prognosis, had turned to this nutritional therapist and was still in fine form several years later. This gave us a certain confidence and hope.

We took a few days' holiday in the Lake District, and Jessie seemed almost back to normal. Her immune system had stayed intact throughout her illness, which we were certain was largely due to the supplements and healthy diet. She hadn't even had so much as a winter's cold. Her skin was beautifully clear, her hair shone, she was walking well, had lots of energy and enjoyed swimming. Her infectious sense of humour was stronger than ever, and she loved the fact that she could so readily make everyone laugh. Then, in the middle of a beautiful walk in the hills, she suddenly went quiet for a few minutes and then said 'I feel wobbly again'. My heart sank: we knew that when the tumour recurred there would be no more conventional treatment – she had already had the maximum radiation possible and chemotherapy was not an option. Trying to pass it off as nothing (as much for our sakes as for Jessie's), we returned home after the holiday to start the new term at school. She was back for one and a half days. So rapid and savage was her deterioration from this point that just two weeks later (by which time she was paralysed on her left side and could barely speak) we arrived at Martin House children's hospice, the very place which I had refused to consider when it was first mentioned.

From the moment we arrived, when we were met at the car in the most gentle, sensitive and welcoming manner, I realised how wrong my uninformed preconception of a children's hospice had been. As we were led to Jessie's room, her name writ large and colourfully on the wall, I began to feel an immense sense of relief that we were in the right place, not only for Jessie but also for Alan, Hannah and myself. There was no more denial, and it felt as though we no longer had to shoulder the whole responsibility for the overwhelming tragedy which had consumed our family.

Although those who have not experienced it will find it almost impossible to comprehend, a children's hospice is by no means a sombre place. Within this bright and homely environment is an enveloping warmth and a freedom just to 'be'; there is practical, emotional and spiritual support when needed; there is an extraordinary and unconditional appreciation of every child; there is wisdom. There is also laughter and joy, for life is celebrated in the moment, no matter what lies in the future. Respite care plays the biggest part in hospice life: children who are not expected to reach adulthood may typically visit for a few days, several times a year, allowing them to form trusting relationships with the staff and giving their parents (and siblings) the opportunity for a break from the 24-hour care which they usually provide themselves. When the time does come for end-of-life care, these have become familiar and protective surroundings.

The hospice cares not only for the ill child, but also for all the other members of the family; and while I stayed with Jessie as we settled in, Alan and Hannah were shown to the comfortable family rooms upstairs. I was acutely aware that Hannah's need for support was enormous – neither Alan or I, nor her devoted but distraught grandparents (who had constantly been there particularly for Hannah since that first, fateful hospital visit in December), had quite enough in reserve to meet her needs. Here she was taken under the wing of a bubbly young member of the care team and she could both be a child again and give some space to the difficult feelings which she didn't know how to share with her family. Meanwhile, the chronic sickness and insomnia from which Jessie had been suffering for the last two weeks or so were eased by symptom-controlling drugs, and she became comfortable and tranquil. She loved being at Martin House and shortly after we arrived she said 'can we come here often?' This was followed, an hour or so later, by 'can we come here regularly?' I am sure that she felt a real concern for the well-being of us, her parents, and she knew that here was a safe place for us all.

Jessie did not languish in bed during these last days. We would get her up each day and she was very much in control of most aspects of her life, choosing what to do, what to wear and what to eat (though she actually managed to consume so little of it). She liked to watch the activity in the kitchen and decided she wanted to bake a cake with one of the care team as a surprise for us. She was too weak to do more than rest her hand on the wooden spoon, but it didn't make any difference to the fact that our strong-willed little girl was directing the activity in the way she wanted, finally decorating what was to be her symbolic last gift with sweets which she had chosen at the village shop and which she bought with money from her own purse. It amazed us that the hospice staff seemed to know her so well and were able to understand her, since she had almost entirely lost the ability to speak and was terribly frustrated by this. I made her an alphabet board, taking a large piece of card and writing the letters of the alphabet on it, along with a number of commonly used complete words. She formed sentences by pointing at these with such alacrity that we had difficulty in keeping up with her.

On 6 May 1994, three days after making her cake, Jessica lay in my arms, the breath leaving her little body for the last time. We stayed with her, in the supportive care of Martin House, until her funeral three days later, and it was during these unreal days that we decided that Jessie's Fund should continue as a memorial to a normal little girl who had lived an abnormally short, but a rich and happy life. In the thick haze of shock, we only knew that the focus would pair seriously ill children with music in some way.

During the weeks following Jessie's death, as we were struggling to find a reason to exist other than for Hannah, I often relived our short time at Martin House. I remembered how busy it had often felt, despite the fact that no more than six or seven children (often with siblings) were ever staying there at one time. There was a constant mélange of sound made up not only of voices but also of videos and tapes or CDs. Jessie had actually been slightly disturbed by this, and once or twice had asked to be taken back to the peace of her own room. What I hadn't experienced at the hospice was any creative music-making, and I felt sure that music could offer the children a uniquely valuable form of self-expression and enjoyment, however complex their medical needs. Although a professional musician, I had only a vague notion of what music therapy was, but I started to find out more about it and realised that a place like Martin House seemed to be crying out for it. On a visit back to the House (bereavement support is an important element in hospice services), I asked Lenore, the wonderful Head of Care, what she knew about music therapy. I was amazed to hear that none of the eight children's hospices in this country at that time had ever had any experience of it. By coincidence (or *synchronicity*, as I view it), one member of the Martin House care team, Cathy Ibberson, was at the point of qualifying as a music therapist and would soon be returning to the hospice. There were no musical instruments there for her to use with the children, and so the first task of Jessie's Fund was clear. I arranged to meet Cathy and we enjoyed choosing a lovely collection of instruments together. Many of them are percussive, pitched and unpitched, with some wonderful instruments from all over the world.

Three months after Jessie died we applied for charitable status for Jessie's Fund, having assembled a board of trustees and written a constitution. It was our aim to enable seriously ill and disabled children all over the UK to access the therapeutic power of music, whether through music therapy itself or through the less defined process of general creative musical experiences. We had witnessed how many children at Martin House are unable to communicate verbally, and we learnt that as many as 85 per cent of children using the services of children's hospices have either lost the power of speech through degenerative illness or have never had it. Martin House aside, there were two hurdles to leap in terms of giving children in hospices access to creative music. The first was simply the fact that neither music therapy nor the use of creative music-making were widely known, and not known at all in paediatric palliative care. The second was the issue of funding. Children's hospices in the UK are not funded directly by the State, so they must raise their huge running costs largely from voluntary donations. We guessed that they were unlikely to spend such hard-won resources on buying in a service about which they knew so little.

The limited funds (and experience) we had available meant that we had to go a step at a time. The first step had already been taken, in equipping Martin House with musical instruments. Our next move was to talk with heads of care of other children's hospices to inform them about the potential of the use of music with their children, and to offer not just the money with which to buy instruments, but the expertise (which we were quickly gaining) in choosing the most appropriate. All with whom we spoke were most receptive, and within a few months we had provided eight kits to hospices around the country.

While we were making some small impact, I realised that the instruments might well be left with a pile of toys or stay tucked away in cupboards if the staff did not feel comfortable in using them with the children, so I looked for a training course which would give them guidance. I could find nothing available, so the only way forward seemed to be to devise such a course ourselves. I had read and been impressed by the book *Music Therapy: An Art Beyond Words* by Leslie Bunt (1994), who is the founder of the MusicSpace Trust and Director of the postgraduate music therapy course at Bristol University. I felt that it would be helpful to discuss my embryonic plans with him. Cathy, at Martin House, thought it was a great idea, and two weeks later she and I were driving down the M5 to Bristol, where we were met by Leslie himself, who was equally enthusiastic about the idea of designing a course specifically around the needs of those who work with children in hospices. Together the three of us started to plan the first Jessie's Fund training course, which took the form of two residential weekends separated by six months. The idea was that after the first weekend the participants would put into practice the skills learnt, and they would use the second session to build on their experience and explore further their own areas of interest.

There was palpable excitement in September 1995, when two or three representatives from each of the children's hospices arrived at Park Grove, the York primary school attended by Jessica just 16 months previously. The head teacher had generously offered the use of the premises for our training sessions. Along with the excitement there was fear: most people had no musical training and during the opening introductions almost all of them said that they weren't at all musical, or even that they were tone deaf. The sessions, with four tutors, were very much hands-on, following the principle that only by enabling care-team members to engage directly with music could they help children to do so. The participants were given the opportunity and guidance to become familiar with the musical instruments and were introduced to methods for using music as a means of communication. They worked in pairs, learning about musical dialogue and gaining insight into how to support someone musically, and they also worked in small groups, creating short pieces.

After the initial nervousness, there was a wonderful buzz for the whole weekend: at the close, beautiful songs from Ghana and Brazil were sung confidently, in harmony, by the whole group. It was difficult to believe that only a couple of days previously some of these singers were claiming to be totally unmusical!

The follow-up weekend, which took place near Reading in the spring of 1996, was intended both as consolidation of the work of the first weekend and as an opportunity for further development. Here the participants continued to explore and develop the use of the instruments (now including electronic instruments[1]), worked on simple keyboard techniques, learnt about the use of vocalisation and singing and looked at musical structure as a framework for improvisation. They were also guided in listening skills, and were taught to consider when to seek help from, or refer a child to, a music therapist. Throughout both weekends there was an incredibly reinforcing sense of camaraderie and mutual support, along with a healthy interchange of ideas between these carers who came from all corners of the country. The format of the course was so successful that it was repeated two years later, and has since become a regular biennial event which is always fully subscribed.

Shortly after we launched our training course Jessie's Fund took a major step forward by establishing the first post specifically for a music therapist in a children's hospice. Apart from Martin House (where Cathy Ibberson had already been employed as a nurse prior to qualifying as a music therapist), no children's hospices had yet engaged music therapists. We became active in encouraging them, little by little, to consider doing so, and in 1996 we offered to fund one music therapy day a week at Acorns, in Birmingham, for one year. The arrangement was not without commitment from the hospice: we drew up an agreement with them that after the first fully funded year we would share the funding equally with Acorns for a further year, and in the third year Acorns would take on responsibility for 75 per cent of the costs while we met the remaining 25 per cent. Thereafter the hospice would maintain the post independently

---

1   These use sensors and switches to harness all types of body movements, from large, uncontrolled gestures down to the smallest finger flex, which can then create an almost unlimited range of musical sounds.

of Jessie's Fund. The project went according to plan, and it was already clear from feedback we received during the first year that the hospice found music therapy an extremely valuable resource, with the therapist welcomed as an integral member of the multidisciplinary team.

Encouraged by the work at Acorns, we began to roll out a pro- gramme, based on the same three-year funding model, of helping more children's hospices to establish posts for music therapists. At the same time more hospices were opening around the country, and we were driven by the knowledge that the management of illness, with its various unpleasant medical and surgical interventions, is the dominant feature in the lives of most of the children who spend time in hospices. Music therapy can provide a vital escape from all this: a place for children to be themselves, to reinforce their identities, to regain an element of control in their lives, to be heard, and to be creative. It can also play an important role in the emotional care of physically healthy siblings, whose needs can sometimes be unavoidably overlooked in the demanding and often draining day-to-day lives of families with life-limited children.

By 1999 we had appointed eight music therapists to children's hospices and I realised that, although I was regularly in touch with all of them, they were each working in comparative isolation in this rather new and specialised field of music therapy with children in palliative care. I saw that they could all gain a great deal by meeting in a forum to discuss their approaches, the challenges and the rewards of their work. I invited them all to a 'network' meeting in York. They came from far and wide, and the day-long meeting hardly seemed long enough to make an impression on all that they wanted and needed to discuss. There was a marvellous feeling of unity in this group of people who were only just meeting for the first time: we immediately had a cohesive team despite the fact that the members lived and worked hundreds of miles distant from each other. The network meetings were then scheduled every six months, with the group expanding as we helped more children's hospices to employ music therapists.

All this activity required considerable financial resources, along with a substantial investment of energy. When Jessie died her fund stood at just over £15,000: I now found a good proportion of my time taken up by fundraising in one way or another. We had formed a Friends of Jessie's

Fund group, which numbered over 200 members, who regularly contributed to the fund. We staged concerts to raise not only money but also awareness, supporters arranged sales and sponsored events and I applied to charitable trusts and foundations for grants. We won the Guardian Jerwood Award for Community Achievement in 1998 – we were by far the youngest and smallest of the five charities to share this prestigious award – with the resulting national publicity winning us many new supporters. This first major public recognition was of huge significance, imbuing us with greater credibility and introducing a wider audience to the power of music therapy with life-limited children.

Our profile was raised further when Victoria Wood, one of Britain's top comedians (as well as musician, actress and writer), agreed to become a patron of Jessie's Fund. She and I had been friends at school, where we were both slight misfits: I had been absorbed by classical music, which went quite against the flow at that place and time, and she was also rather out of step with the average teenager – quiet and shy, but with a sparkling and outstanding wit. We would play duets together, she on her trumpet and I on my clarinet, and both joined the local band. After we left school and went to universities in different cities we lost touch. It was with some trepidation that I wrote to her in January 1999, rather more than two decades later, to tell her my family's story and ask whether she might consider becoming a patron of Jessie's Fund. She replied immediately, saying that although she gets many such requests and has to turn them down due to lack of time, she would be happy to help *us* in this way. Two years later she both presented a BBC television appeal on our behalf and gave a benefit performance to a full house of 2000, enormously increasing public awareness of our work and raising much-needed funds.

Raising money is an ongoing and increasing task, with our work now extending beyond helping children's hospices and into child development centres, hospitals and schools for children with special needs. While we primarily regard ourselves as a proactive charity, following our convictions by initiating the mechanisms for creative musical experiences for children in need, we also receive appeals for information, guidance and funding from organisations and parents all over Britain, and sometimes beyond. There is a limit to how much a small charity can do, and in the long term we hope to bear some influence on the statutory sector. At the time of writing, only a minority of National Health Service Trusts and local education authorities in the UK employ music therapists: most children for whom music therapy could be vital have no access to it or, if they do, it is because their families source their own therapist and find their own funding. Since many parents caring for ill or disabled children have limited earning capacity due to the commitment of caring for their child, it is not uncommon that those in the greatest need are from families with low incomes. Only with persistence and the help of a charity like Jessie's Fund (of which there are very few) is there any possibility of their child receiving music therapy. While we have neither the resources nor the power to provide music therapy on such a large scale, we can lead by example, communicate with statutory organisations and aim to sow the seeds of change.

Despite our increased activities in other settings, there is still a clear focus on children's hospices for the immediate future. We have come a long way. In these early years of the 21st century the number of hospices for children is approaching 30 (it has more than trebled in ten years), for all of which we have provided musical instruments and offered training in music- making. Some of the 20 or so music therapists working in these unique places share aspects of their work with you in the coming chapters.

At the heart of all this, of course, lie the surprisingly numerous children who have faced enormous difficulties with such enduring patience and courage, as did our own little Jessica.

Reference
Bunt, L. (1994) *Music Therapy: An Art Beyond Words.* London: Routledge.

Jessie's Fund CD track
13. 'Searching the Skies' – settings by David Blake of poems by Jessica George (additional track)

Chapter Two

The beginnings of music therapy in our hospice

Cathy Ibberson

Without need of words aureoling my world you smile at my frantic pace to express the inexpressible harbouring my small despairs keeping me new for wonder cradling my song.

'Morning Song' by Christy Brown

Introduction

It is nine years since I returned to Martin House as a music therapist, in the responsible and privileged position of meeting with children and their families. As therapists, we act as a harbour for the emotions the children bring to us, while we too continue on the endless path of self-discovery, seeking the means to express ourselves and comment on the feelings of others.

Martin House

Martin House has a unique setting, surrounded by gardens in the countryside. It is a large and airy modern building, offering families respite and terminal care in a home-from-home atmosphere, and also offering care in their community setting where necessary. The original main house has nine beds, plus space for families to stay. Here families are given emotional and physical support to care for their sick child and siblings in whichever way that is most helpful to them: some families prefer to have a break at their own home and allow us to care for the sick child; at other times they may prefer to stay as a family group. We take our lead from them and follow their daily routines and wishes as far as we can.

There is also a recently built teenage unit next door. This offers six rooms where teenagers can stay, usually without their families. The aim is for a more independent visit, with a looser routine for bedtimes and meals. The unit is generally geared more to meet the needs of teenagers, including themed evenings, outings to restaurants and cinema trips.

My own role as music therapist at Martin House developed gradually over many years.

Martin House, each bedroom opening out onto the garden

My path to music therapy

I originally joined Martin House in 1990 as a paediatric nurse – it had captured my interest when I visited it around the time of its opening in 1987, and I left my name on the waiting list.

I have always been involved in music. My father, a talented accordionist, encouraged me to look over his shoulder at the music he played and, along with my family, I partook in singing and piano lessons and church choirs. Eventually I learnt the guitar to assist with songwriting, and the viola for orchestral playing. I considered a career in music when I was 18, although at this stage I wasn't confident academically. However, I also enjoyed activities in special schools, where I helped out as a volunteer, and had an interest in medical settings/conditions. Nursing became my chosen path.

I loved being on the wards; listening, talking, learning practical skills and enjoying writing essays for exams. I was lucky to be happy and good at my job. Once qualified, I spent time working in caring for the elderly, travelling abroad and enjoying the opportunities nursing offered there, and eventually I took a step further onto the paediatric nursing course, feeling that my niche was in work with children. However, as time passed I found I didn't have a desire to climb the career structure of nursing and, keeping my interest in music going, often brought my guitar and a few other instruments to the patients.

I particularly recall one elderly lady called Florence, who was on a long-term ward for the elderly. During a song session she recalled her days in the WAFs at the time of the Second World War and became very emotional about how her life had progressed, now living away from home after a huge stroke. I felt so helpless for Florence, but realised how the music had opened up her feelings and become a release and outlet for her. We were able to talk further and partake in more song sessions during our time together on the ward, and I began to consider how I could take this skill further within my career. The patients' responses to a simple song or rhythm were so very rewarding, although I felt some frustration at not having enough time in a busy nursing day to pursue this further.

When I was working as a nurse in Dorset, I also used to spend time practising in a piano shop and arranged to have lessons with a tutor in theory and piano. He took me quite swiftly through the Grade Eight exams, giving me renewed musical confidence, and suggested that I study further. I had also by now taken up the saxophone and discovered a love of jazz/blues music, playing in a band. The combination of all these events led me back to a college in Yorkshire which was interested in mature students and offered a contemporary course in music. I was delighted to be offered a place on the degree course a year later.

During this time I was contacted by Martin House and given an interview for a post as a children's nurse on the team. Since I would only have a year to offer them before studying music, they suggested that I work with them full-time for a year and that, during my music studies at college, I join the bank of nurses called in at especially busy periods. This combination of opportunities sowed the seeds for music therapy at Martin House.

I found working in palliative care to be very different from work in general hospitals. The ratio of staff to children was higher and the work more varied because, as a nurse, I followed the needs of the individual child so much more. It also meant that I had to be more flexible in my work, as the team's multidisciplinary roles often overlapped. I would find myself helping with washing and cooking, driving a large vehicle to the cinema or bathing in the jacuzzi, and also giving emotional support to the family of a progressively ill child. These multiple roles gave me the opportunity to offer quality time.

I hoped that my work at Martin House would lead to me using music, and kept it in mind as I enjoyed and thrived musically on the music degree course. I was aiming at a final postgraduate year in music therapy and was delighted to be given a place at Roehampton Institute, near Wimbledon. After overcoming funding obstacles and moving to London for a year (with the help of family, friends and various organisations including Help the Hospices, who paid my fees on condition that I return to Martin House with my skills), I set off on a wonderful, if intense, year to complete my studies, knowing I had work the following year to return to!

Setting up the work and clarifying roles

Jessie had died only weeks before I returned to work at Martin House, this time as a music therapist. I was experiencing great support and enthusiasm from my work colleagues and managers at Martin House, but to have Jessie's Fund's offer of new instruments and funding for my initial supervision, and to meet musicians who had a desire to bring music to these children, was a marvellous springboard for future work.

We were the first children's hospice to establish music therapy, and within my full-time post I initially divided my skills. For two and a half days I worked in the multidisciplinary team primarily as a nurse, and for the other two and a half days as a music therapist. My nursing knowledge of the children and the setting already alerted me to the flexibility required in this work while the dual role gave me a break from the intensity of the one-to-one nature of music therapy.

Being part of the multidisciplinary team as a music therapist felt very important in establishing relationships with the staff and families. At the same time, though, to separate myself from the multidisciplinary team on my music therapy days was complicated. I felt that my colleagues might be puzzled at my having time set aside – and apart – to be a music therapist. Since it was necessary to communicate with the other staff, so they had an understanding of music therapy and my own music therapist's role, I decided to write an informative handout and to hold a workshop during a staff study day. This was a great success and I was reassured and excited by the interest and enthusiasm of the staff. We also discussed the different responsibilities of being a nurse in a hospice like ours, from the overall practical care given and the medication checked and administered, to the emotional stress of caring for a dying child.

The biggest challenge for me was the music therapy boundary and maintaining the privacy of time and space in the work with the children. On the multidisciplinary team of carers (which includes social workers, teachers, nursery nurses and physiotherapists), everyone needs to be open and to share many tasks. For me to do separate and confidential work required us all to trust one another, since we were used to sharing not only information, but were also used to working in the openness of activity rooms.

At the same time, though, having a combined role was an advantage, because I was still a part of the team: I had been a team member as a full-time nurse, and was now as a music therapist. I was able to empathise with my colleagues and keep my nursing skills fresh. I also found that parents had confidence in me during music therapy sessions since, for example, if suction of a child's secretions was required or if a tube feed was in progress, I was familiar with the machinery and the child's vital signs if in distress.

This repositioning of my role(s) and the separation of tasks as well as their overlap was stressful and confusing for a while, but after around six months I felt established. I had a specific room for the instruments and music sessions, my music therapy role and work boundaries felt clear amongst the staff and families and I was more relaxed within myself. A difficult, though useful, lesson was to avoid nursing a child if I knew that I would be working with him or her in music therapy, since this gave us both a clear boundary as to my function. Again this was respected by my colleagues and was rarely an issue.

Supervision was a necessity during the initial stages of my new post and I found a wonderful psychotherapist who helped me rise to the challenges of my dual personae of nurse and music therapist. Most difficult, perhaps, was having no role model or path to follow. The shift from being a nurse to a music therapist required a different focus and meant I had to make very clear boundaries initially, both to clarify the role and to give myself the 'head space' for the emotional needs of the children. I sometimes made mistakes, but had to keep going, convinced I had made an important and worthwhile beginning.

The music sessions

I made sure that everyone at Martin House knew the available music therapy times for individual or group music therapy for children, staff and families. These sessions proved very popular, particularly with the well siblings. I had to prove myself flexible and the open group developed into whatever was needed: story musicals, personal taped song sessions or free-for-all drumming marathons!

Since I knew many of the children visiting Martin House, and also because the care team was helpful in referring children to me, I also established weekly outreach sessions with the more local children. Five of whom attended a local school for children with learning disabilities and I was able to visit a sixth at home.

Sessions such as the ones outlined in the box on the next page were reviewed regularly, to give information to parents and staff, and to consider for how long they would continue.

My dual nursing and music therapy role changed two years later. Returning to Martin House after maternity leave, I knew I would prefer to work part-time. As a second music therapist was engaged during my leave, we were able to work two days each solely as music therapists. To have someone else sharing the role (though we worked different days) was uplifting. We chose to work on a more flexible basis with whoever

Amy, a little girl at the local school, chooses to lead me using her voice to vocalise up and down. She enjoys me playing the saxophone to bend with her, playing extremely high notes right down the scales to the lower register of the instrument. She also responds to the tambourine and likes me to shake it faster or slower as she controls the speed at which we move. Amy gets very excited and loud during these episodes and people outside the room are becoming concerned that she is screaming or becoming agitated. I ask Amy's permission for the headmaster to join us so he can experience the delight and value of our expressive exchanges!

was in the house on our specific music therapy days, since, like many other hospices, Martin House was being used by an increasing number of families, and music therapy was a popular part of the activities and therapeutic sessions on offer. Unfortunately, it became more difficult to organise time for home or school visits as part-time music therapists, and so the outreach service was stopped. At the same time, however, I was growing interested in providing support for the bereaved brothers and sisters.

Bereaved sibling groups

The closed groups for siblings who are over six months' bereaved consist of six Saturday meetings at Martin House and one weekend away over a period of nine months. The children take part in focused workshops, interspersed with fun and creative activities to suit their needs. As a member of the Martin House team, my role is flexible and incorporates a musical session, offering therapeutic skills. This offers the children an alternative means for expression and may involve exploring feelings non-verbally.

One year, some older and musically capable children composed a beautifully moving piece of music based around the feelings they had explored while on our weekend away. We were able to record and keep this for them.

It is the last few hours on our weekend together. We have shared many feelings and now it is music time. Four of the older children are engrossed in composing a piece of music as I look on and become involved in their ideas. Mark (14) is on the piano, and he plays long sonorous melodic chords, sad in their deep bass notes yet hopeful as he reaches the higher octaves of the instrument and intersperses an occasional lyrical melody. Ruth (12) is on the xylophone gliding up and down the keys softly, lost in thought. Kay (13) enters on her penny whistle. It feels like she needs to be heard, the sounds are urgent and shrill. Gradually all the sounds merge and become uplifting, their sentiment entrancing. I listen intently and the rest of the group, seven adults and eight children, are drawn towards us.

Another group of very mixed ages finds a structured session of strong rhythms passed around the group extremely cathartic and uplifting. This led to conducting exercises, where they took turns in controlling the group through loud and quiet episodes, with great anticipation and moments of noisy mayhem!

Some 16 children and adult helpers are seated in a circle. Everyone is eager to hold the instruments as I begin to pass a rhythm around the group. A boy of seven, Adrian, takes the drum imitating my rhythm and laughing. Soon everyone is animated as the sound continues swiftly. I suggest that we all choose from an array of percussion, including bells, wood blocks and shakers, and the rhythm develops, now landing on different beats, becoming colourful and exciting. I encourage Adrian to become a conductor and he stands in the middle of the circle raising his hands to make the sounds louder and down to make them quieter. Adrian loves the control as everyone concentrates and partakes in the exciting group sound. Now other children volunteer to be the leader. David (12), often very quiet and on the outside of the group, steps forward surprising us with his confidence. The music evolves into a further piece as I add my guitar, playing a melodic three-chord bass in C major. People choose other melodic instruments which fit in harmony. The music uplifting and the atmosphere cathartic, we all enjoy this moment. As the music calms I suggest we leave the sound one by one around the circle. The volume diminishes but the intensity remains, until the guitar is left alone. Eventually I fade the sounds and the guitar and we sit for a while, then end clapping one another. We leave the room for our final meal of the weekend together. It feels as though we are warmed in our hearts.

The challenge with the sibling groups is to have a loose enough structure that allows the children to make the session their own. In my experience, groups of children have so much to express emotionally – as well as having the skills and capacities of healthy children!

The challenges

Finally, I want to discuss the challenges of working closely with ill children. During my training as a music therapist a most useful model was the mother/infant approach, discussed by many psychoanalysts such as Donald Winnicott (1965, 1971) and J. Klein (1987). We also spent three months of the training observing mother/infant dyads in their home surroundings, which was invaluable in helping us to think about the client–therapist relationship in our future work as trained music therapists. Esther Bick remarked:

> The central truth one can learn through one's own experience as an observer, and through observing the development of a mother who is learning to be a mother, is directly applicable to the relationship of the analytical couple. It is more painful to wait, to remain receptive and not cut off, to bear the pain that is being projected, including the pain of one's own uncertainty, than it is

to have recourse to precipitate action designed to evacuate that pain and to gain the relief of feeling that one is doing something. (1962, p.233)

Working as a music therapist with children who are losing skills requires patience, waiting, not expecting great leaps or changes and not confusing one's own pace with that of the child. However, the intimacy of a one-to-one musical relationship can bring great fulfilment.

Paul, a teenage boy, lies on his bed. His illness means that I have only his breathing and eye contact to relate to. I sit next to him, with my saxophone on the bed beside him. The room is quiet, and I begin to sing quietly. After a while I am able to synchronise my voice along with the rhythm of his breathing. He seems to be concentrating, and eventually begins to initiate short vocalisations. Listening, I reflect the length and texture of his vocal sounds. As his voice becomes stronger, I pick up my saxophone, bending the sound to reflect his singing. I feel Paul's intense concentration, and the room feels peaceful, our playing intimate.

Endings

As I end my recollections of music therapy's beginnings at Martin House and the children's hospice as a movement, I cannot help thinking about how new this still feels. In our hospice work we deal with many endings, and these can be so bewildering and challenging, especially when, as music therapists, we engage in profound intimate relationships with children who are about to die. As music therapists, we share a conviction that the art of music offers an endless source of communication, and a timeless source of beginnings. And, of course, many of us are parents ourselves.

Michael expressing his enjoyment of the keyboard – I worked with him
in very early music therapy days at Martin House. Photo: Paul Schatzberger

Note

The names of children have been changed to ensure confidentiality.

References

Bick, E. (1962) 'The contribution of mother–infant interaction and development to the equipment of a psychoanalyst or psychoanalytical psychotherapist.' In M. Harris (ed.) *Collected Papers of Martha Harris and Esther Bick.* Clunie Press, Scotland (on behalf of the Rowland Harris Trust).

Klein, J. (1987) *Our Need for Others and Its Roots in Infancy.* London: Tavistock Publications.

Winnicott, D. (1965) *The Family and Individual Development.* London: Tavistock Publications.

Winnicott, D. (1971) *Playing and Reality.* London: Tavistock Publications.

Chapter Three

Music and medicine: Music therapy within a medical setting

Catherine Sweeney-Brown

I have been working in children's palliative care since 1997 and my work has been based in two children's hospices, with initial funding for my hospice-based work coming from Jessie's Fund. At present I work in a rural hospice, which has a large catchment area and provides respite and terminal care for children from a few months old to their early twenties. Many of the children have profound physical and cognitive disabilities, as a result of gradual degenerative conditions; while other children are classed as needing hospice care because the severity of their disabilities reduces their life expectancy. The hospice also has a relatively small number of children suffering better-known conditions such as cancer. My role involves working with the children, their siblings and parents where appropriate, training staff and parents in interactive music-making and providing music for funerals and remembrance services.

Music therapy in children's hospices is very different to that in other settings. Having been taught about the importance of regular, uninterrupted sessions during my music therapy training, the experience of setting up a post within a children's hospice was quite challenging.

In the hospices, I work with children whose physical and medical condition is paramount. My work is shaped by their physical states and I have to address each child as he or she is in the immediate present, instead of thinking ahead and planning my intervention over a period of time. I had to learn the art of flexibility: music therapy sessions have to fit in with rigorous timetables of medication, complicated feeding régimes, doctors' visits and medical procedures. Another complication is that children's responses and engagement in sessions depend on how they have slept the night before, what medication they are taking, what level of epileptic activity or pain they are experiencing at the time of their session, and so on.

Initially I felt de-skilled and hampered by my lack of medical knowledge. I had never worked with clients who were fed by gastrostomy tube, who were oxygen-dependent or who had a tracheotomy. I learnt the mechanics of a tracheotomy the hard way on one occation shortly after I took up my first post: a child looked as though she was about to sneeze, and I quickly held a tissue to her nose, leaving her tracheotomy site uncovered… I had to undergo basic training in some procedures, and needed to become familiar with a bewildering array of conditions and medical terms. Unlike work in other settings, the music therapy sessions had to accommodate things like the need to have a trained nurse present to administer suction, or two large and noisy oxygen machines in the room. Gradually I learnt to time sessions so as to work with as few interruptions as possible, to find long lengths of tubing so that oxygen cylinders could be left outside the music room, to give suction to clear airways if necessary, to position children safely, etc. Also, I began to use music therapy to alleviate physical conditions rather than just making allowances for them.

Working with pain

Although the children attending the hospice have a wide variety of conditions which affect each child differently, some recurring physical problems can be addressed through music therapy intervention. The main one is management and alleviation of pain through distraction and relaxation. Linked to this is the reduction of muscle spasm that is common in conditions such as cerebral palsy. I also find that working with a child's breathing pattern can improve lung function and help to promote a cough reflex, crucial for children needing to expel secretions and maintain clear airways.

The power of music to relax and to reduce perceived pain has been well documented over recent years, with mainstream health care providers such as BUPA recommending its use during labour, medical examinations and operations (BUPA 2003). Music has an extraordinary capacity to distract us from pain. Most of us have musical associations with particular events in our lives, so that certain pieces of music come to have intensely personal meanings. In a study in the *Journal of Pain and Symptom Management*, Bailey (1986) found that when music was used in post-operative care, patients needed less pain relief and had fewer pain reactions. Also, the act of playing music (even as non-musicians) can engage us instantly and powerfully, in spite of our physical conditions, and refocus our attention away from pain towards pleasure. Similarly, music can be used with deep breathing and imagery techniques, to help reduce pain (see, for example, Zimmermann *et al.* 1989; Colwell 1997; Bunt and Pavlicevic 2001).

Since the majority of children in the hospice have profound cognitive disabilities as a result of their medical conditions, it might seem unlikely that they could use music in a focused way to evoke imagery or associations. We cannot explain the power of music to reduce pain in such children in these ways. However, we know that music is perceived by babies before birth, well before they develop cognitive skills. It seems that the ability to respond to music is innate and not linked to cognitive ability. Music's capacity to reach beyond cognitive limitations is what makes music therapy so important in the care of profoundly disabled children.

Music therapist Helen Bonny, the founder of Guided Imagery in Music, also known as GIM (Bonny 1983), shows that music can influence heart rate, hormonal levels, blood pressure, temperature and muscular responses. Put simply, music that has a lively beat and a tempo that is faster than our natural heart rate makes us feel energised, as we respond physiologically to the sounds we hear with raised heart rate and faster breathing. Conversely, slow music that has an even rhythm encourages our heart rate to slow down, promoting a feeling of relaxation. Another effect of listening to music is that music influences the level of endorphins (chemicals that reduce the level of perceived pain) (Miller 2002). These various effects of musical engagement are due to the large parts of the brain that are used in processing music. Both the right and left hemispheres of the brain are involved in processes that are auditory, visual, cognitive, affective and motor, as musical experiences are complex (The Power of Music 2003).

What all of this suggests is that children who are in reduced states of consciousness can still access and respond to music. Before this can happen, though, children need to be as pain-free as possible.

Working with the breath

Pain is often accompanied by muscle spasm and irregular, shallow breathing, and my experience is that, in music therapy, offering music that has a smooth melodic line, a relaxing rhythm and a steady tempo, for example, can encourage the child to breathe regularly and deeply. This helps the muscles to relax, which in turn helps to reduce pain. I have found that low pitched music further increases a sense of security and calm. However, before moving to a more relaxed and regular musical pattern, I often find it necessary to begin by matching the irregular rhythmic pattern of a child's breathing.

Alex is a young boy with microcephaly and cerebral palsy who was born prematurely after his mother sustained a serious fall during pregnancy. He suffers severe discomfort due to his frequent spasms and tense muscles, as well as gastro-oesophageal reflux. He frequently vomits during the night and needs close supervision. Given the nature of his difficulties, Alex has been assessed to be at risk of respiratory failure and is unlikely to reach adulthood. He sits in a curled-up position and takes small repeated inhalations of breath, spending much of the day screaming. I begin by vocalising with his screaming, accompanying this with a low, steady, rocking piano music. Following the contours of Alex's screaming I pitch my voice an octave below his, so that I can mirror his screaming without drowning it out.

He is very distressed, and seems to be unaware of me, screaming continuously. Then I hear gaps in his crying, when he seems to be listening to me, and I also notice that his screaming is following the shape of my vocal line. A sudden spasm triggers further screaming but, despite this, Alex is lengthening and deepening his breathing as he 'sings' with me, and this in turn leads to his unclenching his muscles and uncurling his body.

Once we address his immediate physical need, which is to relax and reduce the level of pain that he is experiencing, we then go on to access the instruments. Alex's profound physical disabilities limit the way in which he can play. However, I discover that when I position him on my knee at the keyboard he plays very loud, angry sounds with great focus, for long periods of time. It seems as though once the initial work has been done Alex can then move from the physical to the emotional level and use external objects and sounds to express his frustration and pain. Sometimes, Alex simply falls asleep once he has relaxed and I have to accept that, as he suffers from disturbed sleep patterns; on these occasions sleep is his most important need.

When singing, we tend naturally to breathe more deeply and use a greater proportion of our lung capacity than we do when speaking and this can be very beneficial, especially for children who do not usually make many vocal sounds. Yoshiko Fukuda (2000), a music therapist working in Japan, has had very positive results working with asthmatic children using singing to improve breathing and to control asthma attacks.

Sally has profound brain damage and visual impairment. She has almost no voluntary movement and her body positioning is poor, as muscle spasm has caused her head to retract so that she permanently looks upwards. As a result, her airways are partially restricted and her breathing shallow and noisy. She suffers frequent chest infections and sometimes requires oxygen.

In our session, Sally lies immobile on her bed while I greet her with a hello song, accompanied by gentle guitar. She takes a little time to engage with what is going on, but first begins to breathe in time to the music, lengthening her breaths to match my phrases and holding her breath to wait for me if I pause. Sally then starts to vocalise softly. Her voice is not loud or sustained but it is in tune with mine and we build up a gentle vocal dialogue.

As well as enjoying sharing a musical conversation with me in this way, Sally also gains physically from her singing. As she breathes more deeply and vocalises, she often manages to cough independently, something that she usually finds difficult. This helps her to clear secretions and maintain her airway without the need for mechanical suction or ventilation.

While the effect of coughing is short-lived, the overall effect of breathing more deeply seems beneficial. The increased level of oxygen in Sally's lungs and the deeper and more regular pattern of breathing promotes a sense of relaxation, and Sally is usually very calm following her music therapy sessions, often sleeping for long periods of time afterwards.

At times, though, music aggravates a child and can be counterproductive. Many of the children at the hospice suffer from severe epilepsy, caused either by brain damage before or around birth, or by a degenerative condition such as Batten's disease or Niemann-Pick disease. Certain sounds can trigger epileptic fits, and this is known as 'musicogenic epilepsy'. Musical sounds that aggravate are usually metallic tones, such as those of wind-chimes or bells. At the same time, though, this is a very individual response, and I have worked with children who do not react adversely to loud noises, but who experience epileptic activity or strong spasms when they hear a soft lyre or guitar. Certain types of brain tumour also cause intolerance of some frequencies, and the therapist must be aware of this.

I worked with James from when he was nine months old until his death at the age of four. He was almost completely blind as a result of his tumour, and he had a highly developed sense of hearing. He was extremely playful with a wonderful sense of humour, and when he was younger he enjoyed musical games and playing percussion instruments, piano and guitar with me. As his tumour increased in size, he began to enjoy the instruments less and less. Also, since the tumour was affecting his hypothalamus gland, he was often extremely hot and irritable, and he experienced severe pain, despite immense levels of pain-relieving medication. Towards the end of his life, the only sound he could tolerate was a gentle, low voice. Our later sessions often consisted of me cuddling a very hot and sticky James and singing softly to him at the lower range of my voice with the rhythm of his breathing while he managed to relax and sleep for short periods of time. His parents valued these times, sometimes holding James while I sang to him, or gently strumming the lyre to accompany my flute playing, and many years later his family still refer to these sessions as positive memories in the midst of a difficult time.

Working with fear

There is no doubt that fear increases the level of perceived pain and that if the fear can be addressed then pain levels can decrease. One of the common fears of children close to death is that they will die alone, and they can refuse to sleep because they are afraid that they will die when asleep without people around them. In music therapy I can be with a sleeping or very still child, singing or playing in order to soothe him, so that he knows that somebody is with him, watching and listening. Working in this way can be useful when a child is in the terminal stage of illness but still conscious and frightened.

David is a young man with Duchenne muscular dystrophy and a mild learning disability. Close to death, he is in a lot of physical pain, needing constant repositioning on the waterbed in the multisensory room. He has not slept for a few days and is exhausted and also very frightened. I have worked with him on several occasions. This morning I ask him if he would like me to bring the midicreator music system to him so that he can play as he lies on the waterbed. We spend a couple of hours playing music together, with him choosing the virtuoso Hendrix style electric guitar sounds that he loves, on the midicreator, and me improvising with him, on flute. Interspersed with these improvisations are periods when I sing and play to David as he watches me or briefly sleeps. Prior to the session David needed repositioning every minute or so, but is now tolerating up to 20 minutes without needing to be turned. As soon as I stop singing or playing, however, David wakes up and becomes aware of his pain.

After lunch, I continue to work with David. He seems calmer and less anxious. In the late afternoon we play a midi guitar and flute duet in a blues style. David's music becomes slower and introverted, sustaining notes around which I play on my flute. Towards the end, he oscillates between two notes a semitone apart, giving a sense of ambiguity and tiredness, compared to the fast scales he played during the morning. I play a semitone above the upper of these notes, so that I can support and comfort him while also acknowledging the tension and not-knowing of the situation with the inherent musical tension of the semitone. We listen together to this dissonance, and then I change to a major third below. This brings our music to a peaceful and contained end. David stops playing and closes his eyes for a while, looking relaxed and calm. I play some gentle guitar to him until he says that he is tired and wants to go back to his bedroom. He dies an hour later.

David's fears about dying are concentrated into an experience of physical pain and discomfort. His need to be repositioned frequently means that a nurse needs to be constantly by his side, and nursing David at this time is very draining physically and mentally for the team around him, as well as for David himself. Improvising music in our work – whether he plays or listens – helps to address his fears in a different way. Once he feels that there is a connection with someone who listens to him on an emotional level he is comforted and his pain lessened.

David was verbal and very shy. As far as any of the hospice staff knew, he never spoke about his illness, and in some way he may have been unprepared for his death. In our sessions that day, nothing was said, but the music seemed to contain all of his feelings and wonderings, and within it he found some peace and relief from his pain and prepared for his death.

Working with beauty

Music-making is an intensely creative experience which involves great beauty. Being creative is healing in itself, as it brings with it a sense of energy and well-being, crucial for children whose physical world is disintegrating. As David Aldridge writes, 'By offering children the chance to be creative then they become something other than patients, they become expressive beings' (1999, p.11).

Mark is ten and has a brain tumour. He has been admitted to the hospice for terminal care: although his tumour has been present for many years, his life has been prolonged by the insertion of a shunt to drain fluid away from his brain. This shunt has now blocked off, leading to pressure on his brain and affecting his speech, vision and ability to walk. The oncology specialist feels that there is no way of safely unblocking the shunt, and that Mark needs to come into the hospice rather than pursuing further medical treatment. His life expectancy is hours, or days at the most optimistic forecast.

I meet Mark on the morning after his admission. He sits in bed, struggling to eat some breakfast because the pressure on his brain causes intense nausea and dizziness. I introduce myself, saying that I 'do music' if he is interested. He says that he is tired, and his father asks if he can come later on if he feels up to it. Later, Mark's father wheels him down to the music room. He chooses to come in on his own and his parents say that they will wait outside in case he needs them.

Mark is surprisingly awake and very keen to play. He seems confused about the choice of instruments and unsure of where to start, but when I suggest that he begins with a drum and a cymbal, he takes the beaters enthusiastically. As I sit at the piano ready to accompany him, I am struck by the alertness of Mark's pose, and this is immediately borne out by the volume and energy of his music. He plays lively music, with a firm rhythmic pattern that seems to defy his physical state: it sounds very much as though he is saying: 'I'm still here!' At the end of this piece, which lasts a couple of minutes, Mark turns to me with a huge smile and says clearly, 'That was pretty good. This must be my lucky day! Let's do another one.' This seemed an incredible statement from a child supposed to be on the last day of his life. I am concerned that Mark might wear himself out, but he insists on continuing.

We play and play for about 40 minutes, with no interruptions. The sheer aliveness and joy of the music surprises both of us, and Mark seems to gain physical energy as he plays. We've recorded our playing and Mark looks very proud as we listen to our improvisations. Finally he admits to being tired, and says that he's going to tell his parents and show them the recordings. I move to push his wheelchair out of the room, but he stands up and walks to the door. I've not seen Mark walk unaided before.

Before leaving work that evening, I go to say goodbye to Mark. He asks if I'll be in the following day. When I say that I won't be back until next week, he says, 'Never mind, I'm going home soon', and asks for the recording to take with him. I take this to mean that he is aware of his impending death and prepared for it. However, when I ring the hospice the following evening to see how he is, Mark is in the swimming pool with his family, and is planning to return home the following morning. The doctor has been to see him and discovered that his shunt has somehow unblocked itself, and the fluid is once again draining away from his brain.

Mark lives a further six weeks, surviving Christmas and the New Millennium celebrations. I continue to work with him weekly at home, building a large collection of recordings of our improvisations. On our last session, Mark is very tired and for the first time does not want to play much music. We are at his home, and he wants to show me the things that are dear to him: his photographs, his toys, etc. He is quite clingy at the end of the session and makes a big ritual of waving me good-bye. He specifically asks me to bring him a tape of all our recordings the following week.

When I get into work the next week, I discover that Mark has come into the hospice the previous evening and is in a coma. I bring the tape around to his parents who are by his bedside, and sing good-bye to him. He dies later that day, never having regained consciousness.

My experience is that children can be incredible fighters and often defy the life expectancies given to them by medical experts. Nobody can ever say how or why Mark's shunt became unblocked that day, giving him another six weeks of life, but there is no doubt that the experience of creating music validated him as an alive young boy, alive beyond the mess and pain of his illness. 'I feel happy when I'm doing music with you,' he says in our second session. In music he found fun and was engaged in something *enlivening and creative*.

Working with silence

One of the unusual music therapy experiences in a children's hospice is being with children who are in reduced states of consciousness. Here, there are few or no overt responses from the child to guide the therapist, and the music is based on micro-responses such as breathing patterns, the flicker of an eyelid or the alteration in muscle tone. It is well documented that people in coma states can retain the ability to hear music and to be reached emotionally by it, and music has been used to help people to regain consciousness after being in a coma state (Formisando *et al.* 2001).

Katie has a diagnosis of persistent vegetative state. Her brain stem is intact, keeping her alive, but she is apparently unresponsive to external stimuli. In our session she is lying on a portable bed. I sing hello to her and then improvise gentle flute music to her. She adapts her breathing to the rhythm of the music and begins to vocalise, crying quietly. Later, I put a midicreator sensor by her leg and she seems to focus on moving her leg to activate the sound.

I cannot say for sure that Katie's responses are linked to my input, or that they are not merely residual psycho-motor reflexes, but it does seem that music can perhaps reach beyond disability in a very profound way.

The 'musical brain' incorporates large portions of the brain and, due to the large range that it encompasses, it can continue to function after other abilities have been lost. It has been my experience that children in reduced states of consciousness, including those with a diagnosis of being in persistent vegetative states, can still respond emotionally and physically to music. The responses can take the form of vocalisations, tears, alterations of breath patterns and movement. Some of these responses can be explained as residual responses that are unconnected to external stimuli, but I would argue that the fact that these children can vocalise to music with accuracy of pitch shows that on some level at least they are processing sounds and responding to them.

The sounds that stimulate these responses seem to be quite specific. I have found that the sound of the flute can promote vocal responses where the piano or guitar do not. This may be to do with the fact that the single melodic line of the flute is easily processed by the brain, or due to the similarities between the timbre of the flute and the human voice. I usually begin by following the rhythm of a child's breathing, playing on her exhalations, and in effect making music from her breath for her. This seems to be an effective way to stimulate children to make their own vocalisations. If a child has even a microscopic range of movement, she can still make music through electronic instruments such as the midi-creator system. However, the challenge when working with children like this lies in the need to facilitate and expect responses, while at the same time not attributing purposeful intention to reactions that are residual. That said, I feel that in such instances it is better to continue to work with the children rather than to assume that they cannot be reached.

Music affects all of us profoundly. It offers physical as well as emotional and spiritual relief when applied clinically and appropriately. Even within the modern and medically sophisticated hospice setting, music has an irreplaceable role in comforting children, working with their pain, their suffering, their fears, and their beauty.

Acknowledgements

I would like to thank the children, past and present, who are discussed in this chapter for being such wonderful teachers. Many thanks also to their parents for supporting my work and allowing me to write about them.

References

Aldridge, D. (1999) *Music Therapy in Palliative Care: New Voices.* London: Jessica Kingsley Publishers.

Bailey, L.M. (1986) 'Music therapy in pain management.' *Journal of Pain and Symptom Management*, 1, 1, 25–8.

Bonny, H.L. (1983) 'Music listening for intensive coronary care units: A pilot project.' *Music Therapy*, 3, 1, 4–16.

Bunt, L. and Pavlicevic, M. (2001) 'Music and emotion: Perspectives from music therapy.' In P. Juslin and J. Sloboda (eds) *Music and Emotion: Theory and Research.* Oxford: Oxford University Press.

BUPA (2003) 'Healthy living: Music for mind and body.' *www.bupa.co.uk/health_information/asp/healthy_living*

Colwell, C.M. (1997) 'Music as distraction and relaxation to reduce chronic pain and narcotic ingestion: A case study.' *Music Therapy Perspectives*, 15, 24–30.

Formisando, R., Vinicola, V., Penta, F., Matteis, M., Brunelli, S. and Weckel, J.W. (2001) 'Active music therapy in the rehabilitation of severe brain injured patients during coma recovery.' *Sanita*, 37, 4, 627–30.

Fukuda, Y. (2000) 'Breathing training for asthmatic children using music therapy and a survey on patient preference in the training methods.' In D. Laufer, K. Chesky and P. Ellis (eds) *Music as a Human Resource: Drafts and Developments. Cologne Studies for Music in Education and Therapy.* Cologne: Verlag Dohr.

Miller, C. (2002) 'An investigation into the use of music as adjunct analgesia with particular reference to the relationship between the effectiveness of music as analgesia and levels of musical training.' MA dissertation, Department of Music, University of Sheffield.

The Power of Music (2003) 'Neurological aspects of musical processing.' *www.thepowerofmusic.co.uk*

Zimmermann, L., Pozehl, B., Duncan, K. and Schmitz, R. (1989) 'Effects of music in patients who had chronic cancer pain.' *Western Journal of Nursing Research*, 11, 3, 298–309.

Jessie's Fund CD tracks

8.   'Evergreen' – Ray (additional track)
10.   'Climb Every Mountain' – Yasmin Harris (additional track)

Chapter Four

A creative response to loss: Developing a music therapy group for bereaved siblings

Jane Mayhew

Introduction

This chapter is based on my dissertation research, as a music therapy master's student. My interest in researching music therapy with the siblings of children in hospice came from my experience within the hospice movement, where bereavement support plays a large part of our care. In the five years since Demelza House has been open, the hospice has had about 330 children referred, of which 80 have died. Each family is offered bereavement support which includes family visits, individual counselling, parent support groups, 'Holding On/Letting Go' grief support weekends for children and music therapy sessions.

We had to devise selection criteria for this particular project, since the hospice covers such a vast catchment area. Because of the limited hospice services in the UK, it is not uncommon to receive referrals regarding support for bereaved children in the community. However, we had to restrict ourselves to children whose brother or sister had been referred to Demelza House and, because of travel arrangements, we chose children living close to the hospice. The sibling's bereavement had to have been more than one year before, because of the nature of the grieving process, which I'll discuss below. Finally, to allow for typical group boundaries, we needed up to eight children within a similar age range. We sent letters to four families informing them of the purpose of the group, enclosing invitation cards to the children. We received three positive responses; the family who declined were moving out of the area. In total there were five children who attended the group.

The bereavement process

Losing a brother or sister can make the world seem like an unpredictable and unsafe place. The surviving sibling may feel out of control and rely entirely on adults for information. Adults often struggle to be honest with children, wanting to protect them from the realities of death, which they think might not always be helpful for the child. For example, not all metaphors used to describe death have beneficial consequences. If a child is told that someone has 'gone to sleep', he or she may become fearful of sleeping.

Child psychiatrist and psychoanalyst John Bowlby researched *Loss, Sadness and Depression* (Bowlby 1998) and showed that grief that is not addressed in childhood will have repercussions in adult life. These can manifest themselves in a range of ways, including adults experiencing difficulties in building trusting relationships, psychiatric illness or under-lying depression and anxiety (Smith and Pennells 1995). Bowlby out-lined four stages of grief in bereavement, with the length of each stage being variable for different people. These stages, in one or other form, accompany all losses and transitions whatever one's age or understanding.

- Phase One of numbing can last for a few hours to a week and may be interrupted by outbursts of extremely intense distress and/or anger.

- Phase Two of yearning and searching for the lost figure can last months and sometimes years.

- Phase Three is a sense of disorganisation and despair, while

- Phase Four is of greater or lesser degree of reorganisation.

Children's response to grief and understanding of death depend on their developmental stage, and Bowlby suggests that 'a child's ego is too weak to sustain the pain of mourning' (1998, p.292).

Bowlby did not restrict his thinking about bereavement to children and suggested that a bereaved adult, too, needs to have 'available a person on whom he can lean and whom is willing to give him comfort and aid…what is important for an adult is even more important for a child' (Bowlby 1998, p.290). Psychiatrist Colin Murray Parkes shows that while the experience of losing a spouse carries risks for adults who are not dealing with their bereavement (Parkes 1986), risks are more difficult to glean in children who have lost a relative or friend (Sood and Weller 1992; Fristad *et al.* 1993).

Joe playing the ocean drum with me: Joe was one of the first children I saw regularly at Demelza House

The children in the group

The music therapy group had five members, Bobby, Andrew, Amy, Victoria and Emily, whose age ranged from six to eleven years (see Table 4.1). Between the ages of six and eight years, children understand that death is irreversible and they may have thoughts and fantasies about how their behaviour, specifically 'naughty' behaviour, is linked towards

Table 4.1: Details of group members

Name	Andrew	Bobby	Victoria	Amy	Emily
Age	11	11	9	7	6
Sex	M	M	F	F	F
Place sibling died	Hospital	Hospice	Home	Home	Hospital
Deceased sibling anniversaries (birthdays/death) during group period	No	Yes	No	No	No
Does the child have a relative in the group?	Sister	No	Sister	Sister	Brother
Known to facilitators?	No	Yes	No	Yes	No
Children's own birthdays during group period	No	No	No	Yes	No

sudden death. From the age of eight to eleven years, children begin to think more about their own future death, which creates its own fears for them. This is particularly relevant when an older sibling dies and the surviving sibling reaches that age. For example, Victoria's older sister died when she was ten and Victoria was anxious about reaching the age of ten and surviving. It was important for us to be aware of the special anniversaries of the siblings' birth and death, as well as the children's own birthdays. Also, the children who had died ranged in age from infancy to teenage years, and their deaths were caused by onset of illness, complications at birth and profound learning disabilities.

Developing this group was quite different from working the more usual hospice sessions, which can often be irregular in attendance and duration, due to the children's medical conditions (Ibberson 1996; Edwards 1999). This pilot group followed the more typical therapeutic pattern: it was a closed group, which took place on a specific day and time. There were ten sessions, each lasting for an hour, over an eleven-week period with a one-week break during half term. Joan, an experienced hospice volunteer, and I facilitated the sessions together.

The sessions took place in an oast room, which is a circular room with a high ceiling, a familiar design within the villages of Kent. Each week we positioned chairs in a circle and the instruments in the middle. These included a clavinova, guitar, metallophone, wind-chimes, various drums (including an ocean drum, a split drum, tom toms and a standing drum), tambourines, bells and shakers.

The sessions took place an hour and a half after school had finished and after most children had rushed to get home and changed. Drinks and biscuits were provided for the children before the group started. This was not part of the session time, and it became quite typical for the children to arrive ten minutes before the session began.

Environmental and time boundaries were in place and adhered to each week and further boundaries, such as confidentiality and safety, were discussed with the children during the first session, as part of the provision of a nurturing and safe environment for the children.

Session 1: Getting to know one another

When the children arrived for the first session, they seemed a little apprehensive and anxious, which is not uncommon for clients arriving for first sessions. Victoria found it particularly difficult to leave her mother and tightly held on to her hand. Perhaps the parents too had feelings of 'anxiety'. We were aware that they might want to protect their children from painful feelings that they thought would be explored in the group. These feelings are often found in parents who have lost a child, as their relationship with the surviving sibling changes and they may want to become over-protective or over-invest in the care of their surviving child.

We said good-bye to the parents and ran upstairs to the music therapy room. The children immediately began to play with the instruments. They hurried around the room, fleetingly exploring the sound potential of the many different instruments. This was the first music that the group made together and it proved to be a non-threatening way in which we could immediately engage with one another. It was also an appropriate starting place, as it demonstrated to the children that this group would be very different from an educational forum, with which they may have been more familiar. It was also an energetic start in which they were able physically to release the feelings of anxiety that were first described.

The children seemed to gather in a circle once they had touched and played most of the instruments. We did not discuss the content of the improvisation as it felt 'good enough' to experience musical group interaction. It was also a way of demonstrating to the group that music therapy offered an alternative form of communication and expression.

We discussed why we had all come together as a group and Bobby immediately replied. In a quiet voice he said 'to think about our brothers and sisters that we lost'. In comparison to his musical playing, which had been dominant and confident, his comment seemed to be dissociated from any feeling. His choice of the word 'lost' led us to think about the difference between losing things and the finality of death. It was also a reminder of how important it is for us to use clear language when speaking about death, rather than choosing metaphors.

The number of sessions were discussed and illustrated in an art activity. Individually, each member drew a calendar, which was divided into ten boxes, to illustrate the ten sessions (Hemmings 1998). This visually confirmed to the children the number of sessions when we would be meeting. It felt important to reinforce this number of sessions with the children, who had all experienced times in their lives when sudden changes had taken place. Any family's routine is very difficult to maintain when a child within that family has a life-limiting condition: family holidays, days out and birthday parties often need to be cancelled or re-arranged due to their sibling's treatment and illness. The children were aware that there would be a break for half term after five sessions.

The session closed with the group sharing a large floor drum, playing and saying good-bye.

Session 2: Who are we?

In contrast to the first session, subsequent sessions began following a more typical pattern with a musical greeting. The tambour was used as the bridging instrument to play and pass to another around the group. Following the greeting, we coloured in the second section of the calendars. The children seemed to feel reassured that we were following the suggestions made in the first session.

During the first improvisation, the children identified with each other through gender, and split with boys on one side of the room and the girls opposite. The musical idea was adapted from music therapists Oldfield and Bean's (1991) 'peace-lovers and warriors', in which the 'peace-lovers' play quietly and the 'warriors' play loudly. The boys were enthusiastic about playing the 'warriors' as they jumped up and down beating the drums, blocking out the girls' music. During the first part of this interaction the girls seemed to be on the periphery, observing the boys playing, and struggling to join in the improvisation. In contrast, the boys experienced this interaction as a very positive time, as they gained attention from the female members of the group.

However, this experience changed when the instruments were swapped over. The girls now played the drums and the boys struggled to make themselves heard, as they were now the 'peace-lovers'. The boys quickly became frustrated and abandoned their instruments and placed them on the floor, perhaps as an indication that the music should stop. At this moment the girls' playing became more disjointed and hesitant, as they seemed to wonder whether to continue or not. They were able to continue playing for brief moments and then also put their instruments on the floor.

Following this improvisation the children seemed keen to reflect upon their playing and spoke about what it felt like to be a 'warrior' and 'peace-lover'. The experience had evoked feelings about frustration, control and being listened to. We wondered whether the improvisation reflected feelings concerning the children's roles within their own families. At the time of a sibling's death, the surviving sibling is con-fronted by the reactions of parents, other siblings and the extended family, as well as his own responses. Where is the space for the surviving sibling to grieve and to whom can he take his grief? Also, bereaved children are often very protective of their parents and may not want to burden them further with their own sadness.

This directed[1] improvisation may have also explored uncomfortable areas for the children, such as dominating the music when they would have preferred to opt for a more passive role. The session concluded with a free improvisation, offering the children an opportunity to choose which instruments they wanted to play. We closed the group as we had begun, by passing round the tambour to each other and saying good-bye.

---

1   In contrast to free improvisations where anything, literally, may happen, directed improvisations are improvisations that occur around a pre-set theme or idea.

Session 3: Fight or flight (Bion 1961)

As soon as the first improvisation began, Bobby and Andrew adopted a repetitive rhythmic pattern (quaver, quaver, crotchet). This strong pulse dominated the music and influenced what the rest of the group were playing. It could be suggested that they had 'paired together' and wanted musically to fight the sounds the girls produced. This may well have been connected with the directive improvisation ('peace-lovers and warriors') used in the previous session.

Andrew's and Bobby's music seemed to be about separating themselves from the girls, to the point of excluding them. When the eldest girl, Amy, tried to join in by imitating the boys' rhythmic patterns, their pattern suddenly changed, leaving Amy to play alone. The volume of Bobby's and Andrew's playing also increased, as if to block out the music the girls were playing. The improvisation seemed to evoke feelings that the girls were not 'good enough' to join in with the boys. The group struggled to work effectively together as the girls musically withdrew (decreasing volume and sound), as if fleeing from the conflict. Bobby also suddenly decided to flee the male side as he stopped playing the drums and physically moved to the opposite side of the room, the girls' side.

I wondered how this would affect the music and whether Andrew felt abandoned by his musical partner. Bobby played with the girls and their music rose in volume, as if strong enough to compete against Andrew. It seemed that Andrew became stuck in playing his repetitive rhythm and overall there was little feeling of group cohesion.

When the group stopped playing, the children seemed eager to discuss what had taken place during the improvisation. Bobby spoke about feeling 'scared' and Andrew commented that he felt that it was 'wicked', adding 'I was all by myself'. He seemed to have gained the attention he longed for, performing to an audience, and described himself as the 'winner'. Victoria commented that she felt like 'giving up' because she could not be heard. Perhaps she could not even hear herself play, and she started to talk about things which she wanted to do, including 'silly' things.

The children became very animated talking about 'silly' things which they wanted to do (for example, dial wrong telephone numbers or have the music on at home on full blast). The need to be 'silly' and do 'silly things' was universal in the group. I wondered whether they were 'all-good' at home and tried to fill the space of the child that had died. They had all seen their parents very distressed and might have thought that by being good their parents' pain would be eased. The children spoke about home life, commenting that some were not 'able to laugh or make any noise any more'.

Being 'silly' may have also been a reaction to Andrew's rigid rhythmic patterns.

We thought about what we could do within the group that was 'silly'. A group scream was proposed and we stood together in a circle and warmed up to scream. First we started with low, growl-like vocalisations, rising to a scream. This was repeated several times. The physical energy and release of this loud group scream seemed to allow the group to feel together again. This vocalisation concluded the third session.

Session 4: Who are we?

Following the previous week's free improvisation, the split and then re-grouping, it seemed important to offer direction for this session. I adapted Kerry Burke's (1991) idea of 'naming an emotion'. For this directed improvisation a number of different emotions were written on pieces of paper, such as angry, happy, sad and frustrated.

Each child chose one piece of paper and then played that emotion on an instrument to the rest of the group. In turn, the group would try to say what emotion they thought was being played. The important part of this musical activity was to offer the children permission for a range of emotions to be explored in the group. What emerged was quite different, as each emotion sounded similar. For example, both happy and sad emotions would be played on the same instrument, with similar patterns and expression. This may have been due to three reasons. First, the emotions were contrived; they did not belong to the children and therefore little feeling was placed upon them. Second, they may have experienced other people, such as their parents, expressing strong feelings and could have been frightened; they may have found ways in which to contain such feelings. Third, it is not uncommon for the bereaved to feel guilty about being happy; perhaps they felt guilty about expressing happiness. This issue was discussed towards the end of this session.

The second improvisation to take place in the session was a 'referential improvisation' (Bruscia 1998). The group members were asked to choose instruments that they felt represented their family members in some way. The instruments could be chosen because of their size, texture or sound. The children worked independently and when they regrouped we found dramatic similarities in their selection of instruments (see Table 4.2).

Table 4.2: A 'referential' improvisation

Instrument chosen	How instruments were played	Family representation	Verbal reflections
Drums, tambours	Slowly, loudly	Daddy's	'Always cross' 'Shouts a lot'
Rainstick, ocean drum, wind-chimes, xylophone	Quiet, glissandos, free-flowing	Mummy's	'Always crying' 'Gets upset'
Keyboard, egg shaker	Precisely, very thoughtful	Sibling that died (sisters)	'My sister used to make sounds like this' (sounds represented in music)
Xylophone, wind-chimes, keyboard, drum	A little chaotic, some quiet	Surviving sibling	None

Following this improvisation and discussion, the children realised that each of them had lost a sister. It was interesting to discover that they were not, unlike adults, preoccupied in discussing what age their sisters were or the condition/illness that they had died of.

The improvisation also revealed how difficult it was for the surviving sibling to explore his or her own identity. This may have been because the children were still discovering their own identity within their families; for example, where they had once been the middle child and were now the eldest. Music therapist Tom Plach (1996) writes that music can 'stimulate verbalisations', allowing the children to discuss issues which they may not have raised within their families. In this group the children spoke freely about the moment when they were informed of their sister's death. They detailed the room they were in, who else was there, who was told first, what time of year it was and what happened next.

It was apparent that the children needed space, both musically and verbally, to express themselves. My approach to the group adopted Esme Towse's (1997) idea that 'playing/talking [ceasing] to become a dilemma' (p.52), and the process of the group was to think in terms of 'Why is this happening at this minute?' and 'What does it mean?'

The children needed little facilitation during this discussion and it seemed that they had universal experiences which they wanted to share with one another. The focus of the discussion was very much on what happened at the time of the death of the children's sisters and seemed to reflect on how the children were able to grieve. They spoke very openly but did not include any of their feelings or emotions. It seemed that the role of music within this group was to help turn, as music therapist Ken Bruscia (1998, p.8) describes, 'frozen emotions...into dynamic forms that live in time'. Due to the limited number of sessions for this group, I also felt it was important for the children to have time to think about the 'here and now' and how life had continued for them since their sisters' deaths. They discussed the very practical issues of home life and the changes that had taken place. This included removal of hoists in bathrooms and unopened Christmas presents.

This discussion led the children to share difficult feelings which they were unable to discuss within their family units. These feelings seemed to connect with the practical issues of home life and the effect their sister's illness/condition had had upon their parents. The children also seemed strong enough to cope with feelings of anger towards their sibling. Amy spoke about her parents' backs hurting because they lifted her sister and she was 'getting bigger and bigger'; Emily said that they did not have stairs in her house because of her sister; Bobby mentioned the amount of time his mother spent with his sister, especially at night; while Victoria seemed cross with her sister as she died near her birthday. I wondered whether she felt that her birthday was now associated with this anniversary.

Ken Bruscia (1998, p.9) states: 'Music can provide a non-verbal means of self-expression and communication or serve as a bridge connecting non-verbal and verbal channels of communication.' The children acknowledged that some things were very difficult to explain and improvising seemed to serve to 'intensify, elaborate, or stimulate verbal communication' (Bruscia 1998, p.9). Below is an extract of Andrew's and Bobby's discussion which acknowledges how hard things are to talk about, connecting this with their understanding of heaven and hell and the reality of their experience.

Bobby: I know why it's hard to explain how you feel, 'cos it's sort of like, it's like to explain sort of, if there's a heaven or a hell.

Andrew: It's hard to like believe that there is a heaven. It's hard to believe that.

Bobby: It's hard to believe like, what has happened is real.

Andrew: Yeah.

Bobby: Or you like try and pinch yourself, to see whether it's all a dream or something, I can't really explain it.

Andrew: It's like you try and wake up but you can't, 'cos she's not here.

The session ended by thinking about how difficult it was to know 'how to be', whether to be happy or sad. I wondered whether they were seeking permission to have feelings which they perhaps found difficult expressing in their families.

Session 5: Sisters

In this session the children decided to give their main improvisation a title. In comparison with the previous sessions, the focus seemed to be placed upon using the instruments as sounding boards on which to express themselves. The title of this improvisation was 'Sisters', which they agreed before playing, acknowledging the significance that each of them had had a sister who had died. This improvisation was the longest one since the first session, lasting over 12 minutes, undulating continually in dynamics and texture. It felt as if the music was going to stop and then it would suddenly restart again and again. As the music developed, the children seemed to pick up on small rhythmic and melodic ideas, a significant change from the music of Session 2.

I wondered whether their individual playing at the beginning of this improvisation was an acknowledgement of their personal grief, which they were able to share and move forward into a group experience.

The group had been reminded of the imminent planned break after they had coloured in their calendars at the beginning of the session, and this may have also spurred the children to begin working more cohesively. When working with this client group, it is imperative to acknowledge the significance of breaks and the feelings of loss which these evoke.

Session 6: Where's the group?

The return after the planned break was difficult, which is not uncommon in group therapy. The session started 20 minutes later than planned, as four children arrived late due to traffic difficulties. There was a very real sense that it had been difficult to return to the group. However, this may not have been solely because of traffic problems.

Perhaps being late gave the children and parents a feeling of regaining control as the group could only start when they arrived. They may have felt angry that the group had not met in the previous week, and had independently arranged a meeting for the children in the play park. It is important to add that the waiting parents, predominantly mothers, seemed to have formed close relationships which developed into an informal support group.

Also, we had not been informed that two of the children, Andrew and Victoria, would not be attending this session of the group. It seemed, therefore, that the focus of the session was on who was not there, a clear reflection of the essence of this group: the absence of their sisters.

The children spent much of the time anxiously looking out of the window, awaiting the arrival of Andrew and Victoria. Again, this may have reflected past experiences in their personal lives of waiting for their sisters to return home from hospital. The music made in this session was fragmented and fragile, interspersed with fantasies about where the missing children were.

Session 7: Reunion

The greeting in the seventh session was full of excitement and expectation, reflecting feelings of the first session. It felt like a reunion, with the children relieved to be together again. It was interesting that the children who had missed the session from the previous week found it difficult to leave a gap in the calendar and coloured in two weeks.

As the group had reformed, the focus seemed to be upon who was now present and how it felt to be back together. We spoke about past issues, such as how their homes had changed, and thought now in terms of what changes had happened to them. Bobby commented that he had now 'changed bedrooms' and Amy said how 'quiet the house was now'. Andrew spoke about changing his breakfast cereal, as he now ate his sister's 'favourite cereal'. It seemed that the children had difficulty associating feelings with these changes and I wondered if they thought about whether their feelings were acknowledged or important. This led to a discussion about feeling guilty when we want to be happy.

I wondered whether adults, and particularly adult family members, are able to comprehend how children respond to grief. During the times of mourning children will also experience moments of happiness and may feel confused about how to express these feelings, especially when they witness how adults, especially their parents, grieve.

It seemed that the children were now seeking guidance and information from us as facilitators, and asked questions which they were not able to broach before. They asked about the differences between cremation and burial. Victoria spoke about where her sister's ashes were in the house. Not all of the siblings had attended funerals and they explored their fantasies about the rituals which they believed had taken place. The facts could be answered, but the focus of the discussion was upon their thoughts about where their sisters now were. Death had suddenly become very real and frightening, as the boys began to think about how bodies rot away. Bobby commented that 'maggots eat away at their face'. While saying this, he visually gestured what he thought happened, as he pulled his skin back on his face. Their understandings of death may have also been influenced by what they saw on television programmes or films.

Victoria and Amy asked if they could bring in photographs of their sisters, and I wondered whether this was a way of making their sisters real again. The group feelings were now very different from what they had been earlier. The rush and excitement had vanished and the group ended slowly by taking turns playing the drum.

Session 8: Where are our sisters?

During this session the children expressed feelings of disappointment and sadness, as there were just two sessions left. It seemed that the children wanted the group to continue, confirmed by Victoria's comment 'I don't want it to end'. There may have been a feeling that the group could be extended in time and therefore extra sessions could be arranged. I felt it was important to stay with the original plan and explore feelings of loss that the group would soon be finishing (Grogan and Knak 2002).

Four members of the group brought photographs of their sisters, following last week's discussion. Bobby had chosen not to bring a photograph and seemed to have difficulty looking at other children's sisters. It was a very brave decision for him to make and led us to think about photographs which are displayed in their family homes.

When looking at the photographs the children spoke about the medical conditions which their sisters had had. Victoria asked why one little girl had a tube up her nose. Andrew seemed to take on a pseudo-adult role, answering the question in highly medical terms and with little emotion. He then commented that 'it must have been really hard for them to die'. I wondered whether there was any space for the children to think about how hard it was for them to survive within their family without their sisters. The group continued to think about how painful it was for their sisters and explored the concept of suffering.

The children requested to play together and spontaneously began a free improvisation. It felt important for the children to have space to do this together, and my role was similar to Siegmund Foulkes's (1948, p.292) suggestion:

> I often felt that my contribution was similar to that of a conductor. I was not producing; indeed I refrained from producing the group's ideas, influencing them as little as I could. But I was nevertheless doing something.

Through playing the children seemed to find some relief from talking. The music sounded quite chaotic, with an underlying feeling that there was a 'battle' amongst the children, trying to find space to be heard. Andrew returned to his repetitive rhythm on the drum and cymbal, which seemed to block out other group members' music.

Moments before the music 'dipped' to the solo keyboard (played by myself) Victoria started crying. Joan comforted her and it seemed the group faced the uncomfortable decision of not knowing whether to continue playing or not. The music restarted when Andrew returned to playing the drum and cymbal. Victoria, who continued crying, did not play but was able to stay in the group. When the music stopped the children reflected on how they felt. 'I couldn't stop. Every time I tried to go over, it was like a shield was blocking me,' said Andrew. His music had clearly demonstrated this. His thoughts of a shield seemed to depict some form of protection; perhaps he had set himself limits as to what he could cope with.

Other children also talked about physical sensations, which could be related to the physical manifestations of bereavement.

'I didn't feel good.'

'Neither did I, I felt sick in my stomach, in my mouth, ugh.'

'I felt chilly.'

Session 9: Exploring indentities

Following the musical greeting, Amy spoke about her birthday, which was in the next few days. The children began talking about who was the eldest in their families and thinking about their position (middle child, youngest child) within the family. This also extended to the wider family unit, as Bobby commented, 'My sister used to be the eldest cousin, now I'm the eldest cousin.' It seemed that the children were now able to explore their own identities.

Following the previous week's improvisation, the children now seemed strong enough to decide whether they wanted to play or observe. Bobby decided not to play and it seemed that others were observing him and playing around him. Although during the improvisation he seemed part of the group, I wondered whether Bobby felt that he could not take part in the playing. This may have been a reflection of his family dynamics; of whether Bobby was able to express his own grief within the family, or whether he observed others and felt excluded.

We took time in the middle of the improvisation to hear children play individually. This seemed to create feelings that focused upon the group finishing soon and individuals going their separate ways. Bobby's eyes started watering. The group music continued around him holding Bobby within the musical framework and sustaining his grief. Again we thought about feelings of guilt and questioned whether the music should have stopped. The children wanted to know why he was upset and asked him directly. Andrew commented that he was 'going to stop, but I couldn't; I felt too embarrassed'. They compared this to times when they had witnessed their parents becoming upset.

The session ended quietly as we passed the 'sleepy tambourine' (Oldfield and Bean 1991) around the group and the children were reminded that next week would be the last session.

Session 10: The final session

In this last session there were similar feelings to those in the first session: feelings of excitement and anticipation about what was going to happen, and some disbelief that the group was ending.

The children asked to play 'peace-lovers and warriors' and seemed able to cope with the roles of dominating the music (warriors) and taking on a more passive role (peace-lovers), a change from the first experience of this improvisation. Following this directed improvisation, I felt that it would be important to evaluate the group and I asked the children five questions. They were given pens and paper and two writers were nominated to write down all of the children's comments. The questions were direct and the children seemed excited to add their thoughts (see Table 4.3).

Table 4.3: Evaluation of sessions

Questions	Children's responses
What do you think this group has been about?	'To think about our sisters'
	'Learn about our problems'
What has been the best part of this group?	'Playing music together'
	'Talking'
What has been the worse bit about this group?	'Talking'
	'Nothing'
	'Making music'
What would you have liked to have done more of?	'More music'
	'More screaming'
What would you like to happen next?	'Come back again, to have more, more, more, but with the same children'

Concluding thoughts

The closing of the group can be viewed as another loss, another bereavement. The group was able to explore and hold these painful feelings within the secure therapeutic environment. The children were eager to share feelings regarding their loss. This was probably the first time that they were able to do this with their peers, outside the family unit. I feel that one of the most important experiences for the children was the permission to explore difficult feelings of their grief in their own different ways. They were given the opportunity (musically and verbally) to exercise a degree of control over their loss, through examining their own identification, suffering and cravings for attention. Loss in all its form is a cardinal issue in all therapists' work.

References

Bion, W. (1961) *Experience in Groups*. New York: Basic Books.

Bowlby, J. (1998) *Loss, Sadness and Depression (Attachment and Loss, Volume III)*. London: Pimlico.

Bruscia, K. (ed.) (1998) *The Dynamics of Music Psychotherapy*. Gilsum Publishers: Barcelona.

Burke, K. (1991) 'Music therapy in working through a preschooler's grief: Expressing grief and confusion.' In K. Bruscia (ed.) *Case Studies in Music Therapy.* Phoenixville: Barcelona Publishers.

Edwards, J. (1999) 'Music therapy with children hospitalised for severe injury or illness.' *British Journal of Music Therapy,* 13, 1, 21–7.

Foulkes, S.H. (1948) *Introduction to Group-Analytic Psychotherapy.* London: Maresfield Reprints.

Fristad, M.A., Jedel, R., Weller, R.A. and Weller, E.B. (1993) 'Psychosocial functioning in children after the death of a parent.' *American Journal of Psychiatry,* 150, 511–13.

Grogan, K. and Knak, D. (2002) 'A children's group: An exploration of the framework necessary for therapeutic work.' In A. Davies and E. Richards (eds) *Music Therapy and Group Work – Sound Company.* London: Jessica Kingsley Publishers.

Hemmings, P. (1998) 'Drawing the boundaries.' *Bereavement Care,* 17, 2, 27.

Ibberson, C. (1996) 'A natural end: One story about Catherine.' *British Journal of Music Therapy,* 10, 1, 24–31.

Oldfield, A. and Bean, J. (1991) *Pied Piper.* Cambridge: Cambridge University Press.

Parkes, C.M. (1986) *Bereavement Studies of Grief in Adult Life, Second Edition.* London: Tavistock.

Plach, T. (1996) *The Creative Use of Music in Group Therapy.* Springfield, IL: Charles Thomas Publishing.

Smith, S.C. and Pennells, M. (1995) *Interventions with Bereaved Children.* London: Jessica Kingsley Publishers.

Sood, B. and Weller, E.B. (1992) *Handbook of Bereavement.* New York: Cambridge University Press.

Towse, E. (1997) 'Group analysis and improvisation: A musical perspective.' *British Journal of Music Therapy,* 11, 2, 51–5.

Jessie's Fund CD track

9.   'Running' – Stuart Wickison (additional track)

Chapter Five

Brief encounters

Ceridwen Rees

Of all the aspects of my work at Helen House, what is most different from any of my other work is giving sessions to a child only once or twice before he or she dies. In this chapter I tell the story of two children, Harry and Alex, with whom I had the privilege of sharing just a moment in time in music, and their responses to it. At the request of Sam and Sarah, mothers to the boys, no names have been altered.

Introduction

I have a fridge magnet at home that reads: 'Where words fail, music speaks.' It was given to me by a very close friend with whom, ironically, I have spent many midnight hours talking! These five little words underpin much of my work as a music therapist. Music has an incredible capacity to reach out and search for the healthy part of an individual, however ill he is, and speak to his very heart and soul. Moreover, I have witnessed the power of music to engage with that person, and enable him to reach out to us in return.

I have always been aware of the effects music has on us. As a six-year-old, when I joined the local village church choir, I could see that our singing moved people. The congregation found it uplifting, sad, joyful – it aided their worship. As a teenager, I remember vividly the effect my oboe playing had on a young blind boy at a children's home. At the end of the concert he could be heard shouting: 'Hoe-bow, hoe-bow, I want to play the hoe-bow!' After he had made many fruitless attempts of huffing and puffing down the oboe, I was about to suggest that he give up, whereupon he produced a sound. He immediately jumped up and began to dance around the room singing at the top of his voice: 'Hoe-bow, hoe-bow, I played the hoe-bow!'

My route to becoming a music therapist was quite a long journey, beginning with a music degree at Kingston Polytechnic. Having graduated, I married and moved to Oxford where, over the next nine years, I built up a peripatetic oboe and piano teaching practice. Interpreting the mood and style of the music is central to my teaching, and this often involves painting pictures in children's minds. Recently a child was struggling to make a phrase sound angry and feisty, and so I asked her to imagine that her younger brother had taken a favourite item of hers. Funnily enough, the music immediately took on an angry, feisty form!

As time went by, I wanted to explore further the notion of how music makes us feel, and how it can be used to capture and enhance or shift a mood or state of feeling. Having benefited from counselling myself by this time, I felt I wanted to 'give something back', but through music rather than words, and this idea led me to embark on a music therapy training course at Bristol University, and subsequently to build up a practice alongside my teaching.

People often find that it is the case with certain jobs that they didn't actively seek them out, but rather that the jobs 'found them'. So it was with Helen House. A misdialled phone number (of all things!) led me to begin work as music therapist there in the autumn of 1998. It is now some five years since I first stepped through the doors of Helen House, which nestles within the grounds of a convent, an oasis in the very midst of the hustle and bustle of Oxford city life. The hospice, which is the first to be established in the world, has recently 'come of age', celebrating twenty-one years of care for children with life-limiting illnesses and their families in 2003.

I have shared over 1000 sessions at the hospice to date, and although I have many poignant memories of the children and families that I have seen 20 or even 30 times, some of the most powerful encounters I have experienced have been with those children whom I have only seen once or twice before they die.

Music therapist Nigel Hartley (Pavlicevic 1999, p.84) speaks of his musical encounters with people who are dying:

> There is a quickness about our work together, because you get to the heart of the matter much more quickly. Our society sees death as a time of giving up, of deterioration, letting go, and here they are, dying *and* being creative and having new experiences of themselves that would have seemed impossible, unthinkable! It's the paradox of working with people who are dying.

Before working at Helen House, all my experiences as a therapist had involved working with clients over a period of several months or even years. My own experience of personal counselling lasted two years, and the high level of trust I developed in my therapist evolved very slowly and over a long period of time.

Faced with a dying child in a music therapy situation, I had an endless list of questions running through my head. How could I possibly achieve any level of bonding with a child when I knew I might see her only once? Could I really make a difference to any child, or her family, in one or two brief encounters? How could I evoke a response from a child or baby who may well be very heavily drugged and offering little or no visible responses?

My questions have found their answers in many sessions over the years, but two of the most memorable and powerful musical encounters are told in the following stories. These are the stories of Harry and Alex.

The smile

It was a lovely sunny, lazy August afternoon as I arrived for work at Helen House. I off-loaded my bags in the therapy room, a purpose-built, light, airy room that is used for both aromatherapy and music therapy. The room is well equipped with a variety of instruments, and it is furnished with a bean-bag, several large cushions and a window seat at one end of the room, giving a very relaxed and peaceful feel to this music space.

Having set up the room ready for the afternoon ahead, I walked down the corridor to the sitting room to be met by a member of staff who brought me up to date with all that had been happening since my last visit. I was told that amongst the families who were staying with us was a mother, Sam, and her 23-month-old son, Harry, who had arrived the day before as an emergency admission. The family had visited Helen House for the first time the previous weekend, but I hadn't met them on that occasion. Harry's older brother and sister, Ollie and Emma, were also staying at the hospice, in one of the four family flats.

We weren't at all sure that Sam would want to bring Harry for music therapy and, since the family were keeping each other company in the quiet room, I decided not to disturb them. I thought that this was all I would ever really know about Harry, and set about seeing some of the other children. If I am honest, I was initially relieved at the prospect of not seeing Harry. After all, what could I offer a dying infant and his mother?

About halfway through the afternoon I did in fact meet Sam and Harry. I was bringing a child back from music to the main sitting room, and saw Sam sitting on the sofa, Harry cradled in her arms. I knew that I needed to introduce myself to her, to say 'hello' at the very least. I have to say that Sam made it very easy for me to be with her, since she was so open about what was happening to her and her son.

Sam began to tell me Harry's story. He had been born perfectly healthy and had remained so up until 15 months of age. Harry then became ill with what was thought to be a virus of some kind. He was floppy and listless, not feeding, and he had lost interest in what was going on around him. Tragically, six and a half weeks later, Harry was diagnosed with a choroid plexus carcinoma, a very rare and invasive brain tumour. Although 95 per cent of the tumour was removed, some 'break-offs' had travelled round his central nervous system and Harry developed a secondary tumour on his spine.

Sam told me that Harry had undergone a battery of chemotherapy treatments, and that his last treatment had been in May, three months earlier. She very calmly and eloquently explained that Harry was now in the last phase of his illness.

I must confess to feeling quite helpless at this point in our conversation. Here was a boy who was dying, and who was on very heavy doses of morphine to control the pain and keep him as comfortable as possible. His capacity to respond to anything would surely be severely limited.

When Sam asked if we could try doing some music with Harry, as he had always loved it, I had to turn my attention to giving this mother and child some kind of musical experience. Sam had made the request and I now needed to make every effort to fulfil it. When I met with her to talk about the writing of this chapter, I asked her why she had been so keen to try it. She said:

> It wasn't just something to do, an activity. It was more a case of wanting to try anything – to use every opportunity to make something of every last minute with my son. Every single moment was precious and meaningful.

Harry had a close connection with music from a very early age. Sam said that he would always settle to the music of Enya, or panpipes, and he always seemed content and serene when listening to music. He used to crawl or bottom-shuffle up to the choir and music group at church on Sundays, and just sit and listen to them singing and playing away. 'It was musical videos of *The Tweenies* and *Barnie* that kept him going through chemo,' Sam told me. 'Story tapes were no good at all! He would even babble and clap along with the videos just weeks before he died, even though he could by that stage do so little.'

As Sam carried her son through to the music room and settled into a bean-bag with him, I turned my thoughts to what I *could* offer Harry and Sam. For a short while, I knew that I would provide them a quiet space in which to be together, away from all the busyness of everyday life in the hospice, and free from the numerous medical interventions that were now such a big part of Harry's routine. Also, despite my nerves, I held on to my absolute belief that for as long as Harry lived, he still had a spirit that could be reached through music. After all, Sister Frances, the founder of Helen House, has a philosophy that the emphasis should be on *living* life as much and for as long as is possible. It was with this thought in my mind that I picked up my guitar, knelt down and began to sing to Harry.

My first song was a simple song of welcome. I sang about what a lovely sunny day it was, and I sang that it was nice to have Harry and his mummy here with me in music time. Harry seemed comfortable and relaxed, and the atmosphere was tranquil and calm.

I carried on singing for several minutes, and then decided to try another instrument. I chose the wind-chimes, sensing that their gentle tones would continue the calm mood that had been created. I was feeling much calmer myself by now, and much more relaxed about the situation I was faced with. If all I provided was a safe haven for Sam and her son for a short while, in the midst of a world which was falling apart, then I would offer something positive. What actually happened gave Sam more than I could ever have imagined possible.

I accompanied the playing of the wind-chimes with some more singing, telling him that this was Harry's special music time, and that Mummy was here with him. I sang Harry the song 'Twinkle, Twinkle Little Star' and began to improvise around the tune with different words, singing gently to him: 'Harry can hear the chimes today, playing, playing all the day.' As I continued singing to him, Harry began to stir. He opened his eyes very slowly, looked up towards his mother and gave her a little smile. I was as amazed as Sam was overwhelmed, and she began to cry gently. We were both very moved at Harry's response to the singing and playing. 'We have chimes at home, he knows that sound,' Sam told me. I was just thinking of choosing some other sounds for Harry to listen to when he was violently sick, and the session ended very abruptly.

I was left feeling a whole range of emotions as Harry was whisked away. First, I was distressed at having seen Harry taken so ill, and found that difficult to witness. I was also sad to think that the session still had somewhere to go, that we might have been able to elicit more responses from Harry. We had, after all, spent only a quarter of an hour together. In amongst all of that however, I also felt extremely privileged to have been part of such a moment. Just at the point in his illness when Sam was beginning to give up hope of any responses from Harry, he had given her a wonderful smile.

Harry died two days later. In a diary entry Sam wrote about how special our musical encounter was. She spoke of 'a very special visit to the music room where a lady sang just to Harry with a guitar, and then played other instruments with and for him. He was still aware and we even had a little smile.'

★

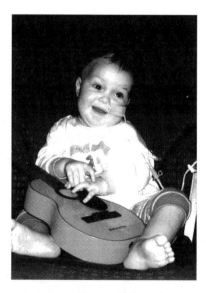

Harry at home with his guitar

My main questions at the beginning of this chapter were: Could I make a difference? Was one session worth it? That music therapy session with Harry lasted for only 15 minutes, but Sam answered these questions very eloquently when we met some months later:

> That was one good moment – the absolute extreme opposite of the horrendous memory of his last breaths. If I didn't have that good and precious moment to counter all the horrific moments, I don't know how I'd cope.

Emma and Ollie

Some good and precious memories of their time at Helen House have stayed with Harry's brother and sister as well. Later that same afternoon at Harry's music therapy session I met Emma and, hearing that she enjoyed dancing and singing, asked if she would like to show me a couple of her dance routines in the music room. Emma was ten years of age at the time, and a bright, energetic girl. Being in music gave Emma the opportunity to first of all be herself. In music, she didn't need to be thinking about how ill her baby brother was or how exhausted her mother was. There could be an air of normality for that length of time. Also, Emma was the centre of attention for a short while. With the best will in the world, much of Sam's time was devoted to caring for Harry, and Emma relished the chance to 'show off' her musical talent! Emma also made up a wonderful game of musical chairs but with the instruments, and Grandma Margaret joined us as well. The whole game caused great hilarity! The pressure was off for a while, and Emma could be Emma.

Ollie, a very lively seven-year-old (as he was then), remembers being allowed to play the drums as loudly as he wanted to. He needed to be quiet around the family home because of his brother's illness, and the drumming offered Ollie an air of normality in what was a very difficult time in his life. Ollie had been sitting in the back of the car with his young brother on the way up to Helen House, when he thought Harry was 'going', but then he sang one of Harry's favourite songs, 'You are my Sunshine', to him and Sam said, 'Harry came back.' These are the toughest of situations for siblings. I do remember someone passing the music room while Ollie was drumming away, and commenting, 'Not so loud Ollie!' I reassured them that Ollie was free to play as loudly as he liked – there was no limit to the volume allowed – whereupon Ollie played even more loudly!

The whole family benefited from their time in music, and Harry's story certainly supports the case for music having made a difference, even in the briefest of musical encounters. The benefits of such encounters are also borne out in my next story, that of Alex.

The dance

It was late in the afternoon, one crisp September day, and I was thinking about putting the instruments away and heading home. I had had a busy day, and seen all but one of the children, nine-and-a-half-year-old Alex, who had spent the day in his bedroom. I had seen Alex just once before, a month or so earlier, in a group session in the sitting room, and he had seemed quite relaxed as I had introduced various instruments to him. Today was only Alex's third visit to Helen House and his mother, Sarah, and two older sisters, Stephanie and Jessica, were also staying at the hospice. They were 13 and 11 years of age at the time. At the beginning of my day's work at the hospice, I was informed that Alex was now very ill, and that he slept for much of the time. It was unlikely that he would be awake enough or well enough for a music session.

Alex was born with a very rare congenital condition, F.G. syndrome. This syndrome is the product of the interaction of two defective genes found in the x chromosome, one each from mother and father. The condition affects males only, although both males and females can be carriers. F.G. syndrome was first described by Dr John Marius Opitz, a German-born human geneticist, and Dr Elizabeth Kaveggia in 1974, when it was found in three brothers and two of their male cousins. Although this syndrome is present at birth, it is not always immediately identifiable. Some common features of the syndrome include poor muscle tone, vision or hearing problems, respiratory problems and learning difficulties. All these characteristics range from mild to severe.

Although Alex always had special needs, he was able to understand quite a lot of what was going on around him. He was able to point to things that he wanted, 'especially the biscuit tin!' said Stephanie. Alex was also relatively mobile and was able to walk, albeit aided, up until seven months before he died.

Sarah told me that Alex also suffered with epilepsy, a condition which often accompanies syndromes such as F.G. The epilepsy wasn't much of a problem when he was younger, but in the last year it had got much worse. He was by now on very heavy levels of medication in an attempt to control his almost continuous seizure activity.

As I was leaving the office having finished my work for the day (or so I thought), I happened to meet Alex's carer who said that Alex was in fact awake. She asked me whether I would I have time to do some music therapy with him after all.

Sarah was keen for her son to have a music therapy session since he had always loved music. Sarah told me that Alex would often have gentle music on to relax him before he went to sleep at night, and that most of his favourite toys were musical ones. Alex would 'bash and hit' them against the floor until they made a noise. Stephanie added that if they didn't make a noise, he would throw them towards her to get her to make the noise for him!

Alex had a lovely cuddly toy Tigger about ten inches tall, that sat up on its hind legs, and would sing when bounced up and down on its bottom. He would spend long periods of time thumping Tigger on the ground until he sang, and then Alex would spin around on his knees and dance with him. *Tigger, The Movie* was the only film Alex ever saw at the cinema, since he was generally a very restless child, and unable to concentrate on one thing for any length of time.

It was not without a small element of trepidation that I went to the music room to gather a few instruments together to take to Alex in his bedroom. I remember that journey down the corridor well. Mixed with a sense of nervous anticipation at the prospect of seeing Alex was the knowledge that I had a job to do and that I was in a position to give Alex a musical experience, even if that meant simply playing for him and on his behalf. I could never have anticipated what actually happened.

Slowly and carefully I laid out a keyboard, my oboe and a few percussion instruments around me, then I picked up my guitar and began to sing a simple 'hello' song. I sang about how good it was to see Alex again. I let him know that this was his special music time, and that his mum was here with us in music time too. As I carried on singing to Alex, I noticed that his eyes began to look much brighter, and his breathing deepened. These responses continued as I did some drumming with him, and Sarah and I felt as though Alex was really beginning to respond to the music. Alex didn't seem to be at all disturbed by the sound and vibrations of the rhythmic drumming or the strong tones of the gong, and so I decided to see how he would respond to some oboe-playing. I have found that there is something about the timbre of the oboe that elicits a response from children who are very ill or who have severe special needs. The oboe has a very pure tone, which often seems to have the capacity to 'break through' when other instruments don't.

I began to play my oboe, picking out an improvised folk melody in a waltz-like kind of rhythm. As I paused to give the music some space, Sarah pointed to Alex's feet. 'Look,' she said, 'he's twitching his toes! He does that when he's happy – I haven't seen him do that in a while…'

I was very touched by this, and started to intersperse my oboe-playing with singing in a similar style:

A – lex is dan – cing, e – ven though he's poor – ly. A – lex can hear, and A – lex can dance. A – lex is hap – py and he can dance to – day!

It was wonderful to see Alex responding so positively to the music, in spite of the levels of drugs he was on to try and contain the fitting and keep him pain-free. I turned to the keyboard to end our session together and I thanked Alex in song for our time together. I sang that I was really glad that he had enjoyed the music, even though he was so unwell. I told him that I was pleased to have accompanied him as he 'danced on his bed'. As I left, Sarah thanked me for our time together in music: 'That was lovely – Alex really enjoyed that, thank you.'

One week later I arrived at Helen House to find a Winnie-the-Pooh mobile hanging at the front door, the symbol that lets people know that we have a child in the House who has died. Somehow I knew it was Alex. Staff are normally telephoned at home when there has been a death in the House, so that we are prepared when we arrive for work, but, with the best will in the world, amongst the busyness of life at the hospice, it doesn't always happen, and so it was on this occasion. I made my way into the music room, hoping that no one had seen me. I just needed some time to have a cry, and compose myself before I could start my work. No sooner had the door closed behind me than it flew open and in burst one of Alex's sisters, Jessica, and one of the care team. 'Oh Ceridwen!' exclaimed the carer, 'you're here, how brilliant! Maybe you can help us?' In hospice work we don't always have the ideal amount of time to process our own thoughts!

'Jessica's Song'[1]

I knew that I would find time to grieve later on, but Jess needed me there and then and I was not about to let her down. The carer then went on to explain that Alex had died a few days ago, and that Jessica desperately wanted to sing something at Alex's service, but that she didn't feel that she would be able to sing live. Would I help her record a song that could be played on the day?

Struggling to control my emotions, I said that of course I would – anything to help. Jessica then told me that she wanted to make a

---

1   'Jessica's Song' is on the CD available directly from Jessie's Fund; see the order form at the back of this book.

recording of her singing with the pop group Hear'Say and their version of 'Bridge over Troubled Water'. When we met to discuss the writing of this chapter, I asked Jess why she had chosen this song in particular to sing. She replied, 'I heard it on the radio on one of our journeys up to Helen House, and I liked the words. The word "weary" stuck out as being a good word for Alex, so I decided on it.' I absolutely agreed with her that it was a good word for Alex, and a lovely thought was that she and her family had been there for him, providing that bridge for him in his difficult last weeks and days.

We put the CD on and I listened as Jess sang along. She was doing really well and, after working on it together for a while, we decided that we were ready to record it. The only problem I had was that the amplifier that I needed to record Jess's voice was at home, half an hour's drive away! In this profession of ours, we all have times when we have to do what it takes in order to 'catch the moment'. I decided that there was nothing for it but to drive home, collect my amplifier and return to Helen House so that we could make the tape (Jessie's Fund CD track 1). I could have waited to do it another day, but for all I knew Jess might not be around another day, or even in the right frame of mind to do the recording. Jess was feeling strong and she was positive that this was what she wanted to do, and now was the right time for her.

At Alex's funeral there were many touching moments, from a reading given by Alex's family, to the playing of the theme tune from *Tigger, The Movie* at the end, but many people commented in particular on Jess's recording. So many people told Sarah afterwards that they were coping up until the point at which they heard that song, 'and then I went'. Jessica's singing enabled people to release their emotions, to have a good cry. Strangely enough (although perhaps I shouldn't be *too* surprised by this!), I described exactly the same response in the opening page of my dissertation for my music therapy diploma in 1997. Time and time again, when people were interviewed after the funeral service of Lady Diana Spencer, they said precisely the same thing of Elton John's rendition of 'Candle in the Wind'. Elton's singing had facilitated their grieving process.

Jess told me a few months later that she was really pleased to have made the recording. 'If it hadn't been for Helen House, I wouldn't have done anything for Alex. This song gave me the chance to do something for Alex.' Jess was also happy because she had wanted a pop group at her brother's funeral, and she had helped provide one! Sarah says it's also something that Jess will always look back on and remember: 'Some memories fade, but this will always remain clear. It will provide a very special reminder to her of her brother.'

But the net is cast even wider than this, because Sarah works part-time in the local pub and one afternoon, some while after Alex had died, the song 'Bridge over Troubled Water' came on over the sound system. Sarah described how everyone in the pub stopped talking, and looked up at her. A few people actually began to cry, but Sarah found herself feeling proud that people were remembering Alex because of that song.

Concluding thoughts

It was at Alex's funeral that Sarah said one of the most touching things that anyone has ever said to me. 'That was the last enjoyment Alex had, in music with you.' Stephanie added, 'You gave him that – thank you.' Both Sam and Sarah spoke of their time in music with their sons with great affection, saying that although I couldn't bring their sons back, no one could do that, I had given them both a very precious memory. Our time in music together gave Sam a smile and Sarah had seen her son 'dance'. Both these children were very close to death, and yet in music they displayed spirits that were still very much alive, wanting to smile and dance.

I believe that sessions such as these offer a great deal to those who are left behind when a child dies. In the very writing of this chapter, the stories of Harry and Alex are told, and the memories of them live on. If Harry and Alex had not been given the opportunity to be part of those short musical encounters, their stories would not be published here.

I am honoured to have been part of Harry and Alex's journey for a moment in time, not towards death, but rather through life.

Reference

Pavlicevic, M. (1999) 'Mary and Steve – creativity and terminal illness.' In *Music Therapy – Intimate Notes*. London: Jessica Kingsley Publishers.

Jessie's Fund CD tracks

1. 'Bridge over Troubled Water' – Jessica
12. 'Celtic Blessing' – Ceridwen Rees, Helen House (additional track)

Chapter Six

'A Bohemian Rhapsody': Using music technology to fulfil the aspirations of teenage lads with muscular dystrophy

Neil Eaves

Since the mid-20th century, music has been a particularly significant socializing factor… Teens find identity, expression of emotions and a worldwide view that is unique to their age group in the music they listen and dance to. The music popular with teens becomes a soundtrack to their coming of age. Music, as a non-verbal, non-threatening modality, can be used by those trained in music therapy to meet adolescents struggling with loss issues where they are, emotionally, cognitively, and developmentally.

Shaller and Rivera Smith (2002, p.3)

The rock band Queen may seem a strange place to begin this chapter but it is where I feel most able to explain why using music technology is often a vital aspect of my work. 'Bohemian Rhapsody' is widely acclaimed to be one of the best pieces of popular music, according to everyone from journalists to the annual 'best records ever' charts that people vote in. However, the song could never be performed in its entirety live by the band as they physically could not do so. The operatic beginning and middle sections were comprised of the four band members recording numerous vocal parts that, when played back together, allowed the music they had in their imagination to be fulfilled musically. It is this analogy that leads me into discussing my work. The client group that I shall discuss often cannot physically perform their work live as they hear it in their minds. Using computers to record each individual part, remove 'wrong' notes or speed up parts that cannot be played at the desired speed allows the music to be produced in much the same way that Queen worked to produce 'Bohemian Rhapsody'.

This chapter will focus on the different approaches I have been using when working with adolescents, in particular the 'lads' (as they are often generically called, and the term I use in this chapter) with muscular dystrophy. As the majority of sufferers are male, this age group can provide many challenges for hospices, which tend to be female-dominated environments. Being male myself certainly plays a role in the dynamics of the relationships with these clients. In this chapter, I start with explaining a little about muscular dystrophy and then about my way of working within the hospice where I am employed. I then present two case studies before reflecting on the value of music therapy with this population.

Muscular dystrophy

Muscular dystrophy (MD) covers a number of similar conditions, each with subtle differences. Muscular dystrophies are all muscles diseases that has two shared features: they are hereditary and progressive. Each form of muscular dystrophy also has its own characteristics. The lads I work with have either Becker (BMD) or Duchenne muscular dystrophy (DMD). These two conditions are very similar, and Becker can be viewed as a lesser form of Duchenne. Both the lads in the case studies used in this chapter have Duchenne muscular dystrophy, and I shall now focus on what causes this and how it manifests itself.

DMD and BMD are due to the gene which enables muscle fibres to make a protein called dystrophin being defective. Those affected with DMD are extremely deficient in dystrophin, while in BMD the deficiency is less severe. At the moment, there is no cure for MD. Usually, sufferers begin using a wheelchair occasionally at the age of about nine years, and become almost totally dependent on it by their early teens. The worsening of disability can be slowed down with physiotherapy and, as the ability to walk is lost, the hands and arms become increasingly important in determining the person's abilities. Joints tend to become restricted in their range of movements. The heart is affected in DMD, but usually without actually causing trouble. When the dystrophic process in the heart does cause symptoms, these symptoms usually respond to treatment. The function of the lungs in people with DMD depends mostly on the strength of their chest muscles, and this usually determines the length of life for affected people, provided that other complications do not occur. When the muscles involved in breathing become very weak, lung function becomes inadequate. Breathing through a face mask used during sleep can relieve the symptoms of drowsiness and lack of well-being.

Aside from the lungs and heart, additional problems can include impaired intellectual development and problems with the joints or the spine. Intellectual disability only affects a minority of DMD sufferers and is not progressive. DMD is fairly predictable. There is a range of severity, and the disability progresses more rapidly in some people than in others. Nevertheless, the range of severity is rather narrow (Muscular Dystrophy Australia – accessed December 2003; this site has a comprehensive guide for parents).

Adolescence

> To deal with terminal illness superimposed on this dynamic
> process of change [adolescence] is a monumental undertaking.

> *Pazola and Gerberg (1990, p.16)*

If you were to compile a list of teenagers' typical worries and then write a list of the typical worries of a teenager who has a life-threatening or life-limiting condition, there would be little difference between the two. Both lists would include items such as wanting to be strong and powerful, wanting to be independent from parents/those in authority, worries over appearance and impressing others and not wanting to stick out too much from the crowd. It is just that, for a teenager who is in the hospice environment, these worries take on extra meaning and can make the emotional journey from child to adult even more fraught.

There seems to be a real polarity within the world of teenagers with MD as, while they grow up emotionally, their physical ability to fulfil their ideas is decreasing and they are increasingly faced with the fact that they are not able to fully realise their potential (see Figure 6.1).

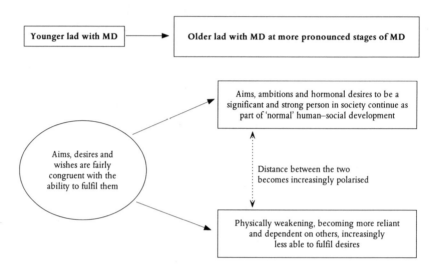

Figure 6.1: Emotional journeys of lads with MD

Teenagers are typically demanding and, understandably, lads with MD can often seem to be more demanding than most. This may be because they cannot be physically forceful and so compensate by making lots of demands, whether reasonable or not. Quite often the lads are booked in for respite stays at the hospice together and can seem like a very primitive bunch when together – roaming in packs, usually having a 'leader' and having lots of in-jokes that make it difficult for the outsider to penetrate the group and join in. Many of the lads who come to the hospice go to the same school, and those who don't know each other at first often have similar interests, such as playing on the games consoles or watching DVDs. Due to regulations, only in certain circumstances can those who are older than 18 stay at the hospice with under-18s, so designated weekends are planned for the older group, most of whom have MD. The idea of having designated weekends is something that other hospices do too, often aiming to help create a sense of community and sharing. It also allows trips such as boating outings or cinema excursions to be easily implemented as the needs and desires of the groups are similar.

Music therapy

As a male music therapist trying to empathise with the lads with MD, I am sometimes rather nervous about approaching them to see if they want to come to a music therapy session, and I wonder how I might feel if someone asked me in front of my mates if I wanted some music therapy. Around the hospice I am simply known as 'Neil, who does music'. I usually bring up the title of music therapy during a first session and I make it clear that the session is confidential and is their space, not mine, for them to dictate what we should be doing. This is often followed by exploring the instruments: I have lots of electric instruments and drums – so much 'cooler' than a triangle or tambourine! However, getting to the stage of the first session is often an event in itself.

I sometimes sit at the table during lunch and talk about football (usually being slated for supporting Newcastle United), play a game on a computer console with them, or watch television together with them. In general, I am just aiming to 'be' for a while. Trust is a big issue and the lads will be very wary of jumping into some deep conversations or improvisations without having had a chance to 'suss me out'. I usually invite them to come and have a look at the music room and have a chat about what music they like. I stay as flexible as possible, but make sure that they are aware that the sessions involve music and time away from the others. Occasionally they will ask for group sessions, but often they seem to appreciate the space away from the others and the fact that they don't have to share me or the time with anyone else. A session might take place during this first visit, or they might agree to come back later that day or when they next come to stay. It is rare for them not to give the instruments a try, knowing that they can finish it at any time. Often, while looking at the instruments, a lad will already have ideas and these will form the first improvisations. It is then a matter of seeing where the music leads.

Sometimes, it can take years before somebody feels able to come to a session, and I always offer sessions to everyone, even if a lot of the lads say no. All children and teenagers surprise us! The toughest-looking teenager who has grunted at me for the past four stays and made me feel awful for disturbing his computer game will suddenly turn around and say that he actually does want a session.

As to what the aims of the therapy are, these are somewhat more difficult to describe. In the words of Cathy Ibberson, 'You move forward together emotionally, yet the body of the child is moving in another direction' (Ibberson 1996, p.26). Within other settings the aims of the therapy may focus on acceptance of a situation and then progress may be possible. However, as clients deteriorate, I sometimes wonder if it is possible to really achieve acceptance since, when somebody accepts where they are, they are no longer physically at the point they've just accepted! To have concrete aims is very difficult, and I wonder if they are necessary at all with this client group. They come to the sessions and produce their music, and my role is simply to facilitate them in doing this. Writing this down seems as though this is not clear therapeutic thinking or that the aims are insignificant. In practice, I feel that there is little else I want to aim towards. The sessions are the lads' and they have so much done for them already that it's important that the aims are decided by them themselves. Often it is only in retrospect that I can clearly state what a session may have achieved.

The music therapy sessions tend to be one-offs, and I may not see a teenager again for weeks, months or even years. Although there is little ongoing work, there is certainly a sense of building on the previous session – as long as the session is placed at where that person is at that time and space. I often have little idea of what will happen in a session, as the lad directs the session to where he needs it to go. Sessions can often begin with neither of us knowing when the session will end. We may have restrictions, such as lunch being ready in an hour or only having an hour due to the number of other young people staying. The sessions end when they end! If we are working on a piece of music, the session may end when this is complete or when there is 'writer's block' and some time away is required.

Conclusion

As oulined in the case study boxes that follow, both Tom and Imran use their music to express and experience emotions that have otherwise been either removed or impaired by having MD. As hard as it is to see such

Tom

Tom is a 13-year-old male who has DMD. He uses an electric wheelchair to move around and is quite possibly one of the most polite and pleasant people I've ever met. His notes state that he is not yet aware of his prognosis – and this is difficult for families to approach. How can there ever be a 'right time' to discuss your son's condition with him, and what it means? Sometimes, hospice staff find out that older lads have told the younger ones why they are in a hospice – with few subtleties. Tom is highly aware and I have often wondered if he does actually know about his condition and is worried about telling his family that he does know, fearing the emotions such a discussion would entail. Nowadays, most teenagers are computer-literate and typing the words 'Muscular Dystrophy' into an Internet search engine gives around a quarter of a million results – I'd be surprised if he didn't know.

Tom is into lots of rock music and like a typical teenager he listens to his music at its loudest, to feel its power. While emotionally he wants to be a strong and fit male who is appealing to women, he has to have his food cut up for him, needs to use straws to drink and has others, usually females, to dress/undress him and take him to the toilet – a far cry from the level of independence a typical teenager would want. His muscles aren't powerful. They continue to degrade, making him gradually weaker and weaker.

When Tom was younger, he learnt to play the guitar but, as his condition worsened, he could no longer hold a guitar nor did he have the dexterity to finger the chords he wished to play. When he first came to the music room, he saw the electric guitar and said that he used to play one, but couldn't any more. I asked if we could experiment with the guitar to find a way for him to play it. I altered the low E string to a D, so that the bottom three strings now were a 'powerchord' (commonly used in rock music). Pressing a thumb onto the fret in a perpendicular line meant that he could play any chord. To overcome the problem of how to support the guitar, we laid it on his knees.

The real beauty of the electric guitar is that not only does it make coming to music therapy cool, it can also be turned up as loud as we want it to be, and it is through his music that Tom can experience what it is to feel loud and powerful. Since that first session, Tom's dad has bought him a guitar and he brings it whenever he comes to stay at the hospice. Tom's condition has robbed him (and will continue to do so) of so many things that he used to be able to do and yet, within his music and the use of his guitar, he has regained part of who he was and what meant so much to him. As Tom continues to make music, he'll continue to grow musically, unlike in other parts of his life.

As Tom's music has become more and more technical and he struggles to play his music all the way through due to his muscles losing tone, I have begun to record his music onto a PC with the specialist music recording software Cubase SX (produced by Steinberg). This software allows the finished tracks to be copied onto audio CDs that Tom can take away. When I work with the lads, music technology allows us to remove many aspects of their condition. They can turn up the volume of the instruments as loud as possible, or record music and edit out the mistakes that might have been made when their fingers slipped. (This is something that not every music therapist feels comfortable with – often due to technophobia!)

Tom composes many pieces, usually one per stay, and I want to focus on one piece particularly. Tom came into the music room one day with different sections for a piece composed while he was at home. Prior to seeing me, he had been playing his guitar with a member of the care team, during which they had developed the musical ideas some more. Tom played me both the sections and we thought about how they could join up together, and then we 'jammed' (played repeatedly with subtle differences) together, him on the guitar and me on the drums. We carried on until he felt happy with his song and how it was going to sound. When we recorded his guitar parts onto the PC, we actually recorded each section about 20 times as none of them were perfect in their entirety, but through technology we cut and pasted them until we had a perfect sounding section that was exactly how Tom wanted the music to sound (Jessie's Fund CD tracks 2 and 3).[1]

Once these sections were recorded and sorted into their correct running order, Tom recorded some drums from the keyboard that were recorded very slowly and then sped up. I added the bass guitar part that was a direct copy of Tom's guitar part but, as he was feeling tired, he asked me to play it. We played around quite a bit with the sections and eventually we had a finished piece which we sped up a little at Tom's request so it really drove and felt powerful and rock-like. When I asked if there were any words, Tom said no, but that it was called 'Everybody Sucks' (Jessie's Fund CD track 4).

Now, I'm sure that if I took that out to someone in the street and played it, that person would have no idea that this was not the music of a regular band, but of someone who has the difficulties that Tom has. A mixture of the retuned guitar and the use of computer to create a perfect recording of the music he wanted to play have removed any musical signs that might indicate that this music has been composed, recorded and performed by somebody who has MD.

I have often wondered why there are no lyrics for Tom's music. He has told me a couple of times that he will go away and work on some words at home but they never get done. I wonder if this is because all the expression is just in music or if he has fears of using words to express matters that he does not feel able or willing to explore. Tom has acknowledged that there could well be lyrics and that someone singing them would sound good. I sometimes feel that creative therapists can over-analyse

---

1   The CD illustrating these examples is available from Jessie's Fund. See the order form at the back of this book.

work, but I have noticed a link to the unspoken truth about his condition within his family and the unspoken words and feelings in his music.

Tom now has a CD of his music that he happily plays to his mates at school or to his relatives at home. While the making of the music allowed him to express many feelings, the actual object of the CD has taken on a whole therapeutic aspect of its own. When Tom plays his music, you can visibly see him sit up in his chair and smile, nodding along to his music, seemingly saying, 'Yeah, I did that and while there may be many things I can't do, I did that, and that cannot be taken away from me.' Cathy Ibberson talks of the meaning of a recorded piece of music, stating that 'the tapes themselves took on a symbolic role as "containers"' (Ibberson 1996, p.31).

As Tom's condition deteriorates, we will have to find other ways to keep music as an accessible form of expression for him, and this is something that I am acutely aware of within this field: I have no idea how someone will present on each visit. Every session is individual and unique, with its own distinctive qualities.

Tom had mentioned performing his music several times and, following a generous donation towards new equipment from a local mayor, and due to some other children/young people (not just lads with MD) also having pieces they wished to perform, I decided to run a concert. After the concert, Tom's mother came up to me and said that while Tom was playing, she was doing everything she could to fight back the tears. She told me that this was the first time she'd seen her son playing like a 'normal' teenager. I've often heard that the hardest part of a grieving parent is not the actual death of their child, but the death of the dreams of what that child could have been. Music therapy seems to allow some part of children to continue to grow when so many other parts of their world are either deteriorating or in stasis.

Imran

Imran is 18, and has given me permission to use his actual name. He was originally to have written a section here but, due to a bout of chest infections requiring hospitalisation, he has not been able to do this. He has, however, told me what his music means to him and I will endeavour to express this as well as I can.

Imran is acutely aware of his prognosis, the fact that he is reliant on so many other people and the fact that without his wheelchair he would have virtually no independence whatsoever. Imran is heavily into dance music and music technology, and the emphasis of our work centres around self-belief, self-expression, motivation and realising part of his dreams. Imran has also composed many songs, usually one per stay, which he records on the keyboard using only one finger, as this is all he can manage. Each song has different qualities and he has discussed the idea that his songs could represent a musical diary of his stays at the hospice, changing from loud, aggressive and 'in your face' dance music to chilled out, relaxed and reflective R'n'B tunes.

As with Tom, I always ask if Imran wishes to name his pieces, as I feel that this can often allow the lads to underline what the music symbolises to them. Also, Imran writes under a pseudonym of 'MC Chuddy Man'. This seems to highlight how he feels when in the music room. Imran can do little for himself – he's fed, bathed, clothed, toileted and transported by others, having to tell people what his needs are. Even if he wants to play the PlayStation, he has to have somebody follow him to switch it on, put the disc in and pass him the controller so that it sits just right in his hands. MC Chuddy Man, however, is an international superstar DJ, who'd be working in clubs, meeting women, making lots of new friends and feeling in total control when on stage, responsible for everyone having a good time, performing his music.

Imran's first session took place in his bedroom as we could not use the music room. When the hospice was built nearly ten years ago, music therapy had not been considered, and the music room I use is next door to the 'quiet room'. This is the room where a child stays once he or she has died. During this first session, the quiet room was in use, and out of respect for the family and child, I moved my equipment into Imran's room. After some initial conversations about who I was and exploring the various sounds available on the keyboard, Imran asked why we were in the bedroom and not the music room. I knew that I had to be honest. I asked if Imran had heard of the quiet room, and when he nodded I said that there was somebody in there. Imran went silent for a moment and I asked if there was anything else he wished to ask. He shook his head and said 'No', but seemed content that I had answered this difficult question well enough.

Imran then directed his attention to the music and said that he wanted to play some 'chilled music'. We spent some time exploring the various drum beats and sounds on the keyboard and he chose a loose-feeling hip-hop beat with a metallic synthesiser sound, quite similar to a vibraphone sound. As Imran only plays with one finger, his hand usually stays around the same area, and he instinctively plays mainly on the white notes, making a concordant sound. I improvised around A minor using the keyboard accompaniment feature. Occasionally he 'strayed' onto the black notes that presented me with a challenge of how to follow this with a suitable chord progression. He seemed to know that these were not the 'correct' notes that he wanted in his piece, and returned to his original A minor improvisations (Jessie's Fund CD track 5).

When we had finished improvising the piece, we listened back to it and I asked Imran if the music had turned out as he had wished it to. He nodded and said that it did sound very chilled and that he was happy with it. I thought to myself that, while it was very chilled, it also had a melancholy edge to it, and wondered if this was a response (possibly from both of us) to our previous conversation regarding the use of the quiet room.

The second and final piece I want to focus on is from the opposite end of the emotional scale and is still being worked on by Imran whenever he comes to stay. The gap between these two pieces is around two years, with Imran staying for a weekend every two months or so. Before we recorded this song, Imran had a very direct conversation with me about what his music meant to him, and this was the first time I'd heard him talk about his condition. He spoke about how motivated he was to record his music and play it to as many people as possible. He complained that he often felt as though people saw his wheelchair first and then him, taking more notice of the things that he couldn't do and having little interest in finding out what he could do. He told me that he realised that his emotions were very much present in his music and that he knew no other way of expressing himself that didn't cause offence and that promoted what he could do when given the opportunity. Prior to this session, Imran had suffered a fall from his chair while in the street alone. Physically, he had lost a tooth, suffered lots of scratches and had a stay in hospital, but the emotional scars seemed to be the ones that Imran felt few people had addressed. He seemed to be confronting the harsh reality of his condition: his only method (the chair) of being mobile had let him down, and he was extremely vulnerable and brittle.

Lads with MD often have great pride in their chairs, decorating them with licence plates and stickers, making them more personal and possibly trying to 'de-medicalise' them. They often race around and know the top speed of each other's chair; they learn to accept the chairs and put almighty trust in them and the security that they provide. However, Imran's had failed him and he was now reminded of how useless he felt at times. These feelings seemed to spark off anger within Imran which he brought into this particular session, complaining of how people saw the chair before him and he was so frustrated at having to rely on so many people and so much equipment. It seemed that he was stating his awareness of how through his role as MC Chuddy Man he could escape this.

When recording the music, Imran wanted to play every note and drum beat. In order to do this, we kept on adding instruments one by one by adding numerous tracks of instruments and making it sound as big and aggressive as possible. Imran also said that he wanted it to sound as though he was actually on stage in a huge club performing this piece, and so we added some crowd noises and he introduced his music as MC Chuddy Man would do if he had a microphone on stage. To do this, I gave him a microphone and he spoke all the words he wanted to say. We added some echo and reverb to make the music sound as though it were 'live'. This song is titled 'Ultimate Bass' (Jessie's Fund CD track 6).

Imran is highly unlikely to perform in a club of such a size but, through his music, he is able to bring his dreams and aspirations closer and make them more real. He has told me that he has played this to his music teacher at school who was dumbfounded. She had worked with Imran for years and never believed it when he told her about the music he was composing.

Music is often temporal. Once played, it is just gone, just a memory. However, once you record a piece of music, it becomes an object and can symbolise many things. I feel that Imran realises that his time is short and, although his body continues to deteriorate, he is still able to be seen and live his dreams and have a fantasy of what life is like outside his wheelchair.

imaginative and strong-willed young people battle to keep their dignity and sense of self while so much of what they can do is wrestled away from them, I do feel that their music remains a constant opening and ability that is available to them. I feel so privileged to share these moments, to see the glint in the lads' eyes when they play their music to others or hear their music back and visibly grow and view themselves as strong and progressive individuals who, momentarily, transcend their chairs and their condition.

I often wonder if any other forms of intervention could offer these lads what the music therapy sessions offer. I honestly feel that there isn't anything that is so accessible and 'cool' that also meets teenagers' needs for support to express themselves as individual and autonomous human beings.

Acknowledgement

I couldn't have done this work with the support of my supervisor, the staff at the hospice and the support of Imran and Tom's family, all of whom I thank from the bottom of my heart.

References

Ibberson, C. (1996) 'A natural end: One story about Catherine.' *British Journal of Music Therapy*, 10, 1, 24–31.

Muscular Dystrophy Australia (accessed December 2003) *www.MDA.org.au*

Pazola, K.J. and Gerberg, K. (1990) 'Privileged communication: Talking with a dying adolescent.' *American Journal of Maternal Child Nursing*, 15, 1, 16–21.

Shaller, J. and Rivera Smith, C. (2002) 'Music therapy with adolescents experiencing loss.' Taken from *The Forum*, Oct–Dec, 2002. www.adec.org/pdf/0211.pdf

Jessie's Fund CD tracks

2. Main riff – Tom
3. Solo riff – Tom
4. 'Everybody Sucks' – Tom
5. 'Chilled' – Imran
6. 'Ultimate Bass' – Imran
11. 'My Heart Bleeds' – Brendan (additional track)

Chapter Seven

The open music therapy group session

Brigitte Schwarting

Introduction

It is a most wonderful and satisfying experience to tidy up after a music therapy group session which has 'gone well'; a session in which every member of the group has participated or been given space to make themselves heard; a session which has had an organic flow of stimulating/invigorating and relaxing/contemplative energy, rather like in a piece of music.

I had seven years' experience of working part-time with children in special schools and with adults with learning difficulties, when I applied for the music therapy job at Francis House Children's Hospice in Didsbury, Manchester. I was one of the very early music therapists appointed by Jessie's Fund. During the following six years I have held many *ad hoc* group sessions there, different from one another, with some turning into concerts or solo performances. I became increasingly interested in looking at what the necessary ingredients for a good music therapy group session might be. In this chapter I share my thoughts and observations about the importance of open group sessions for both the hospice community and the individual and, on a more practical level, let you in to observe one of the sessions.

First, a few words to describe Francis House.

Francis House

Located in light and spacious buildings and surrounded by beautiful gardens, Francis House used to be a Franciscan convent before it was adapted, extended and opened as a children's hospice in 1991. It serves the north-west region of England and is in contact with over 150 families and an increasing number of bereaved families. There are seven beds and five flats for families to use, if they choose to come with their child.

The existence of Francis House stems from the belief in the sanctity of life and respect for the dignity of the person. Saint Francis of Assisi is said to have had an exquisitely human element in his character which enabled him to meet people with an all-embracing sympathy. It was his constant concern to respect the opinions of all and to hurt the feelings of none. He is the role model for serving the sick and the poor. His all-encompassing view of the world, where life and death, the sun and the moon, the water and the air and every creature belong to the whole and show the presence of God, remains very meaningful for Francis House today.

Francis House offers residential care to children and their families, which means that a child or a young person can have a certain number of short stays (between three and five days) per year. Some families choose to book their children in for a longer period of time while they go on their annual holiday. It also offers care for children in their homes and terminal care in-house.

My work at the hospice includes many different things: individual music therapy sessions, staff training, involvement in education days and workshops for parents, and also playing the organ at the Rainbow Day Service (an annual remembrance day for bereaved families), funerals and other services. It entails involvement in the 'Shining Stars' programme (for bereaved siblings), in the 'Seasons' programme (for pre-bereaved siblings) and in other activities, such as organising regular short pre-lunchtime concerts at the hospice (in collaboration with Chetham's School of Music and the Royal Northern College of Music), putting together a tape library for the sensory room, compiling a songbook, and indeed...holding *ad hoc* open music group sessions. These sometimes happen spontaneously, when there are enough children in and about, or when members of the care team ask for them specifically. However, for a long time now, Wednesday afternoons have been set aside for possible group sessions.

The traditional music therapy set-up for a 'closed' ongoing group with a handful of selected children over a period of time did not seem possible, given that the likelihood of my meeting the same mix of children on two visits is almost zero. And yet I was convinced that a music therapy group session had enough to offer both to the ill children and to the hospice community. In group sessions, children experience being together with others, making peer contact, forming friendships and working together. Thus these sessions offer a rare opportunity for children and youngsters who can be very isolated because of the severe nature of their disability or their history of long hospital stays. The group session can help reduce anxiety for those who are new to the hospice, and also provide an opportunity to play. If we remind ourselves how important play is in the development of a child, how together with movement/motion it is the most important prerequisite for learning, we will understand that many of the children and youngsters who come to Francis House have a lot to catch up on.

It is really important to provide a structure to these group sessions (a greeting and a good-bye with a sequence of songs, improvisations and pieces in between), and to take on a very active role as group leader, being at the centre of the group, explaining in brief words what a song is about, deciding on the repertoire, handing out instruments to individual children and observing them closely. This enables the members of the group to trust the situation and to trust me.

The initial challenge was to find the right place for the sessions to take place. After attempts to use the chapel (too spiritual) and the music room (too tiny), the lounge end of the big central dining room was chosen. It is spacious, with sofas, an upright piano and a wall-mounted television. It is also a very central place in the building, *en route* to the downstairs bathroom, soft play area, jacuzzi, multisensory room and the flats or, in another direction, towards the chapel, rainbow lounge and back office. People coming in from outside can see and hear us from a distance! (The children's rooms upstairs, the conservatory and the smoker's lounge enable them to get out of earshot if needed.) There is enough room to put children and youngsters in a semicircle around the piano in their big adjustable comfy-chairs or wheelchairs or even in a bed with members of staff between them. But why not come along and witness today's session?

The open session

After sitting through the staff 'handover' at two o'clock in the staff room, I approach the lounge. Everything looks bright and white because it has been snowing. Christina, the co-ordinator of the late shift, who is walking with me, says that they have built a beautiful snowman during the course of the morning, and asks if we could sing the snowman song in the music group. I can hear someone wailing in loud bursts of high siren-like sounds. Oh yes, I recognise this sound: it's Bettina, the 16-year-old girl with Rett's syndrome. She wears her obligatory earphones and Adele, a member of the care team, is fiddling with the tape in the machine, because switching the tape on always calms Bettina, as we keep being told. In the past, when I had individual music therapy sessions with Bettina, she cried a lot, and it is quite a relief to see that she also cries outside the therapy room. Bettina looks at me briefly when I say 'hello' and tell her about the music session which we are going to have in the lounge in a little while.

The rest of the children and staff are having a restful time after lunch. The big sofa, a two-seater of truly royal dimensions, has Patrick lying on it at one end. A member of staff, Claire, is next to him, holding up his feed tube. Patrick, like so many other children who come to Francis House, can't be fed orally, but has to have special food straight into his stomach. He looks so much better than last time when I saw him in his bedroom. He still has an oxygen mask over nose and mouth, but he greets me with his eyes, even makes a sound when I say 'hello'. We know each other well from countless sessions in the music room or up in his bedroom. He keenly vocalises and has spent the occasional session on top of the grand piano on a sheepskin rug in order to feel the vibrations of the lower notes. With his severe cerebral palsy he is prone to frequent chest infections, which make him very ill. He is 15 years old and spends most of his time in a horizontal chair on wheels, moulded to the shape of his body. I have a lot of admiration for Patrick. He expresses a strong will and personality in his small and dysfunctional body.

At the other end of the sofa is Charles, a 14-year-old with San Filipo syndrome, slouched right back and almost lying down. As always he has got his hand in his mouth, but the bib he is wearing is dry; Sister Freda, who looks after him, points out how well his medicine has worked in stopping his dribbling. I tell Charles jokingly that he'll have to wake up and do some work soon, when the music starts.

In one of the (very colourful adjustable) zoo chairs is ten-year-old Emily, another girl with Rett's, who comes to Francis House. She looks at me through her glasses with big eyes and sighs. The other zoo chair is empty: maybe Charlotte is being changed at the moment.

I walk through the glass doors at the opposite end of the lounge and along the long corridor past the fish tank, the snooker table, the jacuzzi and on through the empty adolescent lounge until I reach the music room. I put down my bag and give in to the inviting look of the piano keys, playing a few chords of something going around in my head. I get the manuscript paper with the not quite finished song out of the cupboard, the 'Triangle-Tango'. Playing through it, I feel nervous with the thought of using it for the first time in a group session, and also quite pleased: it has some Argentinean feel about it. I won't use it in today's group. None of the children here today will hold a beater, let alone a triangle and beater. On another Wednesday this could be entirely different. I rearrange a pile of photocopies and come across various sheets which I brought back from London during a seminar week. Amongst them is a very lively rocky 'Let's Make Some Music' song, written by one of my fellow students. How could I forget about these three songs? What was the other one? Oh yes, a kind of singing game: 'Is There Someone Here Called David?' Playing through that one on the piano, I realise that I'd have to know it much better in order to use it; it is amazing how out of control the fingers can get on the keys when the focus is not only on playing but also on the members of the group and how to project one's voice, singing and looking inviting and encouraging.

In my head I go through today's children: there are Bettina, Patrick, Charles, Leo (whose name I read on the board for the bookings, but who was not in the lounge, when I came through), Emily and Charlotte – an unusually big group. A group of non-verbal children only. A group of mainly teenagers, with the exceptions of Emily and Leo who is six. I will try the new song 'Let's Make Some Music', which has a more serious, more grown-up tone than the younger, more playful 'Listen To...', which I use a lot. I start putting instruments into the box to carry into the lounge: lollipop drum, tambourine, triangle, cabasa,[1] maracas, bells, hand chimes,[2] claves,[3] drum sticks, and the standing drum and cymbal.

Through the corridor window I can see the beautiful snowman with his hat and scarf.

When I arrive in the lounge I find that the staff have already set up a big circle with the children, including the sofa with Patrick and Charles. What a pleasant surprise! It has not always been like this: sometimes in the past I would arrive with all my instruments and find the lounge deserted, with some people out at Tesco, others having taken their child upstairs for a change or the doctor on call having suddenly arrived to look at a child. Life in the hospice is only slightly predictable and 'plan-able'.

Charlotte is in the second comfy-chair, and who should be sitting on the floor cross-legged right by the piano but my special friend Leo! Leo has a genetic illness with very complex needs. He usually has very exuberant individual music therapy sessions, in which he sings and plays the piano with me. However, outside the music room when we meet, Leo looks away, purses his lips and plays 'I-don't-like-you'. I am always puzzled by that reaction, which earns Leo a great deal of laughter from staff. Is he punishing me for something? Have I disappointed his expectations in the past? Does he feel his sessions under threat? It is not until the first greeting song is sung that his face starts to radiate with a big smile and he begins to sing in his very own way: a fairly low note, which he holds for the length of an exhalation and which he varies a little bit in

---

1   A percussion instrument with chains of beads around a resonating body which is a kind of pumpkin in the ethnic form or a rough metal cylinder with a handle in the commercial form.

2   Unlike conventional chime bars that require two hands to play, hand chimes, which sound similar, have a kind of beater attached and can be played with one hand.

3   A pair of wooden sticks.

pitch as the chords of the song change. The more excited he gets, the louder he sings.

I sing 'Oh Good Afternoon', a gentle and warm greeting song, with a verse for each child, and two or three members of staff sing with me. There are some keen singers among the staff at Francis House: Diane, a passionate and experienced singer and concert-goer, will even stay on after her work shift to take part in the session. The staff's own enjoyment creates added dynamic to the sessions. Others have had to overcome some degree of shyness to join into the singing, while some would probably never dream of opening their mouths. It is nice to see how the focus and expectation wanders from child to child. Emily, when sung to, looks up and is very aware, smiles but hardly ever responds; Charlotte, the pretty 12-year-old with cerebral palsy, predictably responds by vocalising on the note D. In many a session with her in the music room, I found that she always sings back on that note, which is why I chose the key of D major for the greeting song. Patrick's face is completely hidden by Claire, but she indicates to me that he realises and enjoys being greeted in the song; Charles, propped up into a more upright position with the help of two big cushions behind his back, responds by doing his loud claps, which I answer back from the piano with short and loud chords. And my friend Leo? He can't take his gaze off me. Bettina sits on the little sofa with a member of staff on either side. Her earphones have come off and she seems settled and happy again. Susie, a new member of the care team, is holding her hand and supporting her. Susie keeps looking at me in a way which makes me feel a little insecure…what are her thoughts at this moment, I wonder?

The instruments are laid out on a little coffee table with the exception of the reed horns and the hand chimes, which I keep at the piano. They are an invitation, even a temptation, for staff and children alike, so without much ado we hand out instruments and sing the grasping 'Let's Make Some Music' with a good pushy beat. The first verse is 'Listen to Everyone' and I use it to look around and see who is doing what.

Listen to everyone…

Ana, the Spanish volunteer, is on the floor by Leo. She has given him the lollipop drum with a beater, but he is throwing both away. When she gives them back to him, he throws them again. Instead he reaches for a small pair of claves, just the right size for his little hands. Leo used to have a pair of purple Early Learning Centre maracas with him at all times. They are nowhere to be seen and his interest in the claves is a new thing. He plays fast and continuously with tremendous pleasure.

Christina helps Emily with the cabasa, holding the instrument and placing Emily's hand over the beads. It needs a bit of persuasion and gentle coaxing to stop her constant hand and finger movement and to open up her hand. She enjoys the sensation on the inside of her hands as the beads 'tickle' her. She looks at Christina, also at me, holding her breath as she does so, but she won't attempt to make a sound on the cabasa unaided.

Sharon is helping Charlotte play a tambourine by tapping it lightly against the insides of her wrists or pulling it along under her fingers. She signals to me that Charlotte is a little unsure and doesn't tolerate the touch. I reduce the accompaniment to one beat per bar and indicate to Sharon to follow these slower beats.

Bettina has got the standing cymbal in front of her and beats with a stick in bursts of three or four beats at a time. She rocks her upper body backwards and forwards slowly, smiling happily.

Claire fetches a triangle for Patrick and herself, and plays it for him, near his face, where he can both hear and see it. As a music-lover and someone who likes dancing, she is very supportive in these music sessions. Charles is holding a maraca and moving it about and, when he drops it, Sister Freda puts it back into his hand.

After the first verse, everyone has their own 'Listen To...' verse sung to them and another in which we don't sing but listen to the instrumental playing which that person is doing accompanied by the piano. I try to go from one to the next according to who is ready to play and who is paying attention. After having made up my mind to let Bettina play, the phone goes and Susie, Bettina's helper, leaves her in order to answer it. It will be interesting to see what Bettina does on her own. I start the verse, pausing after Bettina's name and making eye contact with her. After two 'empty' pauses Claire, who sits with Patrick, rushes in to help and lightly holds Bettina's hand around the stick, moving her arm over the cymbal and dropping it onto it. I wish she could have waited longer and given me a chance to try some musical means to stimulate Bettina's playing.

In order to hold the attention of everybody present, I want each verse to sound a little different and personal. So I play fast in a higher register for Leo, loud and with strong accents for Charles, very gentle and smooth for Emily, with a rocking rhythm at a slower speed for Bettina, in a different key for Charlotte and, for Patrick, I play with the hands spread widely on the piano keys, using very high and very low notes. Charles has become a little restless and has got to his feet. Sister Freda is taking him for a walk around the lounge.

I feel reminded of previous group sessions, when there have been several mobile and active children who did not stay in one place for long and I felt like a shepherd, or rather like a mother hen wanting to keep the chicks together. Today this is not an issue, because only Charles is restless and, after a little stretch, he is back on the sofa for more music. Today's session is also different from those when a teenager in an electric wheelchair hovers in the background, seemingly uninterested, wanting to see what is going on but not wanting to be seen doing it.

An Israeli tune

I want to continue with something energetic; something that brings everybody together... An Israeli tune, which has a 'getting-faster section' in it, is the answer. I hand out all different drums and tambourines available and start playing. Sharon and Claire laugh expectantly, because they recognise the tune and know what's coming. The piece starts with three strong beats and a rest in the steady and slow section, followed by an exhilarating wild tune which gets faster and faster. Leo is vocalising on high notes and I join in on 'La-la-la'. Sharon, Claire and Christina are clapping in time and Sister Freda is dancing with Charles. Susie keeps looking at me without any expression. She must think that I am mad.

Everybody gasps and lets out a sigh; it feels like getting your breath back after running a 100-metre sprint. 'Again, again, again' is what little children would say, and I never play it just once. So here we go again, the slow and sober beginning, then the tumultuous race into total chaos and noise as some players, Bettina and Leo, translate the stimulation from music into fast, uncontrolled drum-beating. The third time round, everybody knows what is happening and waits for the tempo increase in order to let rip.

As we are playing, Arnold, Charlotte's older brother, walks in. He has just arrived from school and still wears his school uniform. He throws a bag on the floor and comes straight up to me and asks for the guitar, which I haven't brought. I tell him where to find it in the music room and he sets off to get it.

'Three Bells'

Now is a good moment for the 'Three Bells', a beautifully still and intimate song, which uses three hand chimes, a little one, a middle one and a big one. I love using the hand chimes. Their sound is warm and pure and hardly ever fails to focus the group and the player. For the three players I choose Emily, Patrick and Charlotte, because neither of the last two can move an arm to play a drum or a cymbal, but they can hold onto the 'beater' of the hand chime as the helper bends it back and they can feel the tension of the spring and the release when the 'beater' flicks back and the chime sounds. It is a bit complicated to get the angle right and Sharon is assisted by Christina, another member of staff, to help Charlotte successfully. After a general 'Listen to the Bells', I sing 'Patrick's bell ring-ring-ring-ringing, Emily's bell ring-ring-ring-ringing, Charlotte's bell ring-ring-ring-ringing' and again 'Emily's bell ring-ring-ring-ringing' as the harmonies change and the children play their own distinct bell notes.

Arnold comes back strumming an out-of-tune guitar, and I ask him to hold on just a minute, while we play the song again. He kneels down by his sister and wants to do it for her. I ask him to watch her do it instead. He picks up the guitar again and sneakily strums the strings. How hard it is to just listen, especially if the music is slow! At the end of the song I ask Arnold to pass me the guitar in order to tune it into a harmonious minor chord, not the real guitar-tuning. It means that he can now strum along to a song without having to play the chords.

'El Condor Pasa'

After collecting the three hand chimes I ask everybody to listen to Arnold play the guitar and start playing two alternating chords with a right hand tune on the piano. Arnold strums along, steadily and with great dedication. As we are playing together, a tune comes to mind: 'El Condor Pasa', a melody from the South American Andes about the big bird, the condor. I play it and while Arnold keeps on playing his chord, there is an almost magic silence in the room. The slow pace and the long-held notes suggest a feeling of gliding gracefully on top of the world… The applause for Arnold is inevitable, and he wants to play it again, and after that again and again. I persuade him that twice is enough, while in my head trying to decide which of two songs to do next: there is 'Pass the Bells', a bit of a circle game, or a clapping song I wrote, which Charles in particular enjoys. A bit of action is needed, something which involves everybody. The clapping song wins.

Clapping song

I play and sing it. Some of the care staff recognise it and join me singing. It has a pattern of two claps alternating with two rests. How wonderful to have as many as four or five members of staff in the room. Six actually, because precisely at this moment Josie, my wonderful colleague from the bereavement team, is walking past, no, dancing past with a big smile on her face and clapping in time. After three verses I carry on singing, but leave the piano and go round the circle, 'visiting' each child and clapping or tapping their hands lightly, and clapping my own hands loudly in the two rests, like an echo.

Charles engages quite well: we do a whole verse, whereby he does his own clapping at 'Charles speed' and I adapt to it. Patrick gets the tapping variation on the backs of his hands, while Bettina is offered my open hands to clap into. She does it twice and then withdraws. I move on to Charlotte and tap her hands, and start a new verse with Emily. I take one of her hands into both of mine, then hold it with my right hand and clap onto the back of it with my left hand. Leo does not want to let go of his claves at all. He taps them rhythmically at the right speed, so I sing 'tap' instead of 'clap'. Back at the piano for a final verse of the song with chords, I look around and notice that Arnold has lost interest and has wandered off, and Leo has shuffled up even closer to the piano now; he is almost touching my legs. A quick glance at the clock shows that there is time for one more song before the good-bye. Maybe the 'Woodpecker', using all the instruments with a wooden sound, or something lively and focusing for everyone to join in like 'What Shall We Do With the Drunken Sailor?', 'Oh When the Saints', 'Charlie is My Darling' or the 'Drum and Cymbal Song', which needs two players one after the other or...oh no, there is the 'Snowman Song' to do, I nearly forgot. I start the rippling D minor chords introduction and then we sing 'I'm Walking in the Air'. If there is any more text than this, I don't know it. The usual dilemma...

We end the song and somebody keeps on singing loudly: it is Leo. Without much thinking, I accompany him in D major and make up a very sober, march-like 'Who Can Sing Bye-Bye?'. Now that Leo is singing continuously again, I realise how quiet he has been during Arnold's guitar-playing and the 'Three Bells'. As we go round the circle the staff encourage the children with gestures and words to sing 'bye-bye'.

More notes

The timing is just right: we finish the session at five past four. Little Leo still can't take his eyes off me. 'How can you not take him home with you?' says Sharon to me. As I walk back with my box of instruments, Arnold catches up with me and asks whether he can do his song again in the music room. We play it through with the piano in the music room and I tell him the title and where it comes from. Then it is time to take notes about this group session. One thing is certain: this group in this constellation will not happen again; it is a unique event. It started, went on and finished. Will it have any effects on its members' lives beyond this afternoon? A children's book called *Momo* comes to my mind, in which the author Michael Ende (1985) describes how the time of all human beings is stored up in the 'flowers of an hour' in a time safe. Each flower differs in shape, colour and design, existing for only an hour long, during which time it transforms from bud to flower, wilts then dies. Thinking of this makes me realise how precious and special the group sessions are, how we celebrate a moment in time when we are together, create music and communicate in that universal medium: music.

On reflection about today's session the first thing to note is how supportive and focused all the staff have been. I have held enough sessions where the amount of chatting seemed to outweigh the amount of music.

The real star of the session was Leo, who not only managed to take part very successfully, playing his newly discovered instrument, the claves, and singing, but also listening to others when it was not his turn. His enjoyment in the session was so obvious to everybody present, which proved the point I kept making to other members of staff, who were fooled by his displaying the cold shoulder towards me.

Arnold's solo performance fitted in rather well. I am glad that he took an interest, got involved and found something to do which was obviously meaningful to him. Musically the song 'El Condor Pasa' provided a nice contrast to the lively, rousing Israeli dance, something to lean back and listen to, rather than to do.

Charles did very well in clapping for a whole verse of the clapping song. He was able to concentrate and the close one-to-one relationship with his helper helped with that.

And Susie? I wonder whether with time she will be able to join in and enjoy a music group session.

It is vitally important to give enough support to each member of the group in their role with an open mind, to observe and record their response as starting points, and to recognise change. Over a longer period I have come to know most of the children in their roles in the group session. In many cases, our individual sessions helped me to get to know their musical language and their favourite instruments, and also how to help them use an instrument.

When I came across the article 'Music therapy as milieu', by the Norwegian music therapist Trygve Aasgard (1990), I was reminded of my Wednesday afternoon sessions at Francis House. He speaks of 'music environmental therapy' and how 'music therapy enters the open spaces of institutions' (p.33). The picture of the big lounge-cum-dining room where the music sessions take place emerged, with the cook or the kitchen volunteers poking their heads through the food hatch occasionally to watch a group or whistling along with a catchy tune, with the phone ringing at suitable and less suitable moments during the session (sometimes in the key of the music, more often not), with the passers-by (whether visitors, parents, members of the administration or the fundraising office) stopping for a moment and looking on encouragingly, or smiling with delight or falling into dance step.

It is clear that such a group session brings a focal point to the hospice community at that moment in time because it can be heard and will draw curious people who want to see what's going on. It involves everyone as equals and gives the care staff a chance to sit down together and be part of a creative live music experience, in which their own personal engagement is asked for just as much as that of the children.

In this way the music therapy group sessions can take on an almost experimental quality: we explore how to be together, how to help and yet not get in the way.

When a number of children and members of staff assemble for a session around the piano, the hard work on-shift is interrupted for a joint activity – there is a sense of identity, of belonging together. It can be very relaxing too, because there is no policy about how to interact in a music session or how to handle musical waste or musical products. Rather refreshingly, little needs to be taken into account concerning health and safety during a music therapy group session (with the exception of the cleaning and sterilising of mouthpieces). There is all the more room for our souls to come to the fore and expand.

As music therapists, our aim is to 'compose' the group session from the beginning to the end with contrasting elements, variety, and inclusion of all the 'voices'. If we bring with us into the session enough energy to motivate the group, enough power to focus its members and enough luck for the external factors to be favourable, then we should be able to tidy up with satisfaction after a 'good' music therapy group session.

References

Aasgard, T. (1990) 'Music therapy as milieu in the hospice and paediatric oncology ward.' In D. Aldridge (ed.) *Music Therapy in Palliative Care.* London: Jessica Kingsley Publishers.

Ende, M. (1985) *Momo.* London: Puffin Books.

Chapter Eight

Living community: Music therapy with children and adults in a hospice setting

Graeme Davis

Introduction and scene-setting

We all have a desire to understand and make sense of our lives. Through reasoning and questioning we attempt to gain a more meaningful experience of life. The process of understanding my role as a music therapist in a hospice for children and adults has forced me to reflect on and try to make sense of a variety of experiences. These experiences have raised many questions: questions relating to immediate concerns, such as which music, which instruments or which musical approach is needed for the session I'm about to undertake? And more philosophical questions: how can I understand the role of music therapy with the dying when the range and needs of the people I meet are so diverse? Is there a commonality within such diverse working environments and client groups?

Pasque Hospice

I've been working at the Pasque Hospice for two and a half years. The hospice accepts both adults (Betty Robinson House) and children (Keech Cottage) in two linked self-contained buildings. The age range at Keech Cottage is 0 to 18 years, sometimes extending to 20 years. This wide age range is because diagnoses include degenerative conditions, often with associated learning difficulties, which means that the transition from child to adult status is complicated. There have been very few children with cancers. Generally, these children seem to be kept within the hospital setting and then discharged. This may be due to their being in remission or being discharged home to die, where the hospice community nurses may then be involved.

The adult hospice is for people aged 18 and upwards. While anyone with a terminal or life-limiting illness can be admitted, the majority of patients are mainly suffering from cancer. However, other diagnoses include motor neurone disease, multiple sclerosis and heart disease. The hospice is split into two areas, a ten-bed in-patient unit, and a day care facility for up to 20 people a day, open four days a week.

The diversity of my role and work situations is enormous because I accept referrals from both adult and children's hospices. This chapter recounts a working day in the form of a diary, and I hope to highlight some of the differences and similarities that I have come across when working with children and adults in the two hospices. Through this diary format, I also explore the uniqueness of music and how it can reveal our common humanity.

A day in music therapy

8.00 a.m.

A sunny, calm Friday in late spring. The birds are singing in the trees, only punctuated by an aeroplane taking off from Luton airport in the distance. A beautiful day to be alive!

I go into my office wondering what the day has in store. Since I began working here I've learnt that no day is ever predictable – one of the joys and challenges of being a music therapist at a hospice for children and adults! Pre-planned sessions don't always happen: unexpected referrals, dramatic changes in health, hospital appointments, all help to make planning very difficult! Despite this, I have three scheduled slots. I've requested a session at 10 a.m. with a baby I've seen earlier in the week. She showed small responses to music and I want to explore this further.

I've also arranged for this session to be videoed.[1] At midday I've got a group relaxation session with the adults in day care, and at 2.00 p.m. one of my regular ongoing sessions with Peter in his 60s. Outside these times I am free to fit in sessions with either children in Keech or adults in the in-patient unit (IPU).

I check emails, have a coffee and then I'm off to Keech and the IPU for updates on their patients.

9.00 a.m.

I use my swipe card to open the security door into Keech. The unit is quiet, with bright colours and toys everywhere. Along the walls are pictures of happy children on visits to the seaside, children sitting in Porsche cars, art works... On another wall is a big coloured placard with pictures of all the hospice's children, both the living and the dead, set within a frame of a star. I pause, looking at the pictures. Memories of some of them come flooding back. I go into the nurse's area for an update. Referring to the problems I had yesterday with a dodgy circuit on my keyboard, one of the nurses says, with a twinkle in her eye, 'How's your organ?' 'All the better for seeing you!' I reply.

Apart from good peer support and external supervision, one of the most important coping mechanisms here is humour. Indeed, in a recent speech to hospice volunteers, the chairman of the trustees said, 'The Pasque way is with a smile.' In the midst of so much sadness and sometimes tragedy, there is always a place for smiles and laughter.

Many Keech children have congenital birth defects that involve progressive conditions over months or years and which threaten their lives. Initial hospice stays are usually for a few days at a time, as and when requested by parents/carers. An initial relationship can then develop between the child, their family and the hospice. As the child's condition progresses, stays can become extended and/or more frequent so that,

---

1   Video recording enables closer evaluation of non-audible responses, aiding a more complete understanding of the client. It can also be used to show work to parents/guardians and members of staff.

when the need for terminal care is reached, the child, family and hospice staff are all familiar with one another. All of this means that every music therapy session needs to be a complete entity in itself. This is different to the adult side, where day care attendees may come regularly for some months or sometimes years. Even on the IPU, stays are usually for a week with a re-admission perhaps a month or two after the initial discharge. Sometimes clients are discharged into day care.

★

Back in the nurses' area, I'm told that baby Lucy has not had a good night and is sleeping at the moment. Immediately I reschedule times in my head. 'How about 3.00 p.m.?' I ask. 'Fine – oh, and by the way Mary's coming in at 10.00 a.m. today. Can you see her?'

Mary is in her early 20s and has Down's syndrome. Her speech is very unclear but she is very outward going and generous with her affection. Despite being over the official age for Keech, it is more appropriate for her to attend Keech than the adult section. 'OK, how about 10.30 a.m.?'

I leave Keech and make my way to the IPU. Between the children and adult hospices there runs a long corridor, skirting round the outside of the hydrotherapy pool. It forms a definite break – and bridge – between the two areas. The IPU is very bland compared to Keech. The colours are all very pale and only a few pictures hang on the walls. Generally it's quite quiet, punctuated by strains of gentle music coming from a central area or from a patient's room. I report to the nurses on duty. I'm told of an elderly gentleman, Mike Jones, who's near to death. His family is with him and the nurses, hearing that he had a musical past, thought the family might like some music. I'm introduced to them. Mike is lying in bed, coming in and out of consciousness. His wife and their two grown-up children are by his bedside. They tell me, briefly, of his love of music and how he helped their children to learn to play the piano, and request some music by Bach or Chopin. However, one of the daughters has to go to visit her husband who tragically has just been admitted to hospital with a similar condition to her father's. Not wanting to intrude, I take my leave, arranging to return later in the day.

As I continue on into the day care unit, I'm thinking ahead about what kinds of music to offer them: what would be appropriate, possible choices that are graded in emotional intensity, etc. My thoughts are interrupted by another quip about my dodgy organ.

10.00 a.m.

Friday in day care is 'young person's day' – people under 50 years of age. I generally have some regular clients who like to come to the music room for individual sessions. However, at the briefing meeting,[2] I'm told that the attendance for today is low, because of illness, effects of chemotherapy, hospital appointments, family commitments, etc. Most of the attendees are of the age where they have young families, with a great many commitments and associated pressures. Music therapy offers them time to explore their own experiences within music without necessarily having to express them in words. However, since my individual clients are not in, I will only offer the regular group relaxation session.

10.30 a.m.

I return to the music therapy room, a large, quiet room initially constructed as a chapel/multi-faith space. It is about 30 feet by 20 feet with a vaulted ceiling about 25 feet high. The room has wooden floors, and windows on two sides. There is sufficient space to have the instruments spaced out and still be able to run round the room!

12.00 noon

After the dynamism of Mary and the large music room, as described in the box on the next pages, I'm now in day care: a large carpeted room in an L shape with pale pink walls and a white, quite low ceiling. In one half of the room, armchairs are arranged in a semicircle with the piano in front and slightly to the left. The other half of the room is a dining/activities area leading to treatment rooms. The four adults sitting in the armchairs are quiet, tired and look poorly.

The relaxation session has been offered following specific requests. Most people's experience of music is one of listening passively and, for

---

2   This meeting is quite structured and formal and is to update not just me but also the volunteers and complementary therapists who are working in day care that day.

most, active music-making ends when they leave school. Many people find listening to music deeply relaxing and gain significant benefit from it. The session is designed to offer a quiet space for people to be at peace with themselves and their thoughts – an opportunity to be caressed and cushioned by soothing, supportive musical sounds. One of the participants has past experience of meditation and uses this during the relaxation session.

Mary enters the room accompanied by the play specialist and a health care assistant (HCA) as well as an oxygen cylinder. Immediately she gives me a big hug, her usual greeting to familiar people, and then goes straight to the drum kit. She picks up two drumsticks and begins to beat the drums. I rush over to switch on the tape recorder and then go back to the keyboard to accompany her.[3] She finds a moderate speed and beats in a basic pattern within two beats in a bar. Her beats are loud, deliberate and energetic. I improvise in a blues-style sequence that relates directly to her beats. She begins to sway her body to the music and stops suddenly, requests a microphone and begins again. This time she sings as well as beating the drums. The words are unintelligible, her pitch is mainly monotone and her tone somewhat harsh, but she is fully committed to her song! She begins to change the quality of her sounds and varies her dynamic, becoming softer. All the time she maintains the relationship between her singing and her drumming while being aware of my supporting music.

Her facial expressions change. She's now centre stage, performing her song, singing her heart out. She makes a sequence of melodic lines and then repeats them. I immediately offer this

3   All sessions that involve active musical participation are tape recorded. Tape recordings form a central part of the musical/therapeutic process, and also help to communicate the work to other professionals. They can also be used for educational purposes, provided ethical clearance is obtained.

again to her. She's aware and immediately responds, developing the sequence into a new musically expressive idea. By now she's gesticulating to the play specialist and the HCA to join in, initially via small hand-held instruments and, later, via dancing. She has now instigated a complete backing band and dance troupe. The session becomes increasingly lively and not just for Mary. The two 'supporting artists' are dancing up and down the music room, intermittently being given further instructions by the soloist. Amongst the puffing and panting, there are smiles all round. Despite her obvious limitations Mary is experiencing herself fully as an equal person, sharing and leading a musical experience with three other people. She's alive and vibrant. All four of us share in this musical experience. Seeing the exhaustion beginning to appear on the faces of my colleagues I begin to wind the music down. Mary is immediately aware and responds. She ends the song. Incredibly, we've been making music for 50 minutes. We were all totally unaware of the time passing.

The session begins with my usual setting of session boundaries and guidelines for the session (relating to the length of session, sitting comfortably, closing eyes, and focusing on the music etc.). The music has a moderate speed, movement and level of sound, and gradually winds down to being very slow and quiet. The music comprises of both composed piano music and improvisations. No familiar songs are used as they can have all kinds of memories and associations for people and this might distract attention from the gradual relaxation process. Generally the response is a gradual relaxation often culminating in sleep. The musical content is one of ever-increasing simplicity and space, and after 30 minutes the session ends. A brief period of silence is held in which the participants engage again with the world around them.

Feedback for this group is regularly sought and comments from participants have included feeling rested and calm. Overall, the session has
proved to be very popular, with some participants able to reach deep
levels of relaxation.

★

So far in Keech, passive listening has only been offered to tired and/or
fractious babies in order to soothe them and help them to sleep. In those
situations my approach is to ask a nurse to gently rock the child in his or
her pram or, if the child is very distressed, for him or her to be held. I
improvise lullaby-style music with gentle wordless singing. Interestingly,
although the social setting and choice of music is very different, the
observable response of both adults and babies to the musical experience is
similar – one of relaxation and inner peace.

Generally the emphasis for music therapists is to encourage their
clients to participate actively. However, passive experience has an important place within the therapeutic possibilities of music in the hospice, and
brings into play concepts such as a creative offering from one person
being received by another, as well as the listener's associations and relationship to particular music/sounds. How the listener receives the music
and/or perceives the music informs the therapist of the potential therapeutic journey.

2.00 p.m.

I meet Peter at the entrance to Keech. 'Hi there, hairy,' he says, making
reference to my receding hairline. 'God, you don't get any better-looking
do you?!'

'Good afternoon Peter and it's good to see you too!' I reply. We have a
laugh and then I take him to the music room in a wheelchair. Peter is 60
and is articulate, humorous and intelligent. He has no musical background as such, although he used to go dancing with his wife in the past.
Starting from a somewhat sceptical view towards music therapy, he has
continued to attend individual sessions for about 18 months. Peter uses
the sessions as a means of personal exploration – not especially via discussion of his musical experiences (although, inevitably, he does talk
about his music-making) but via the actual experience of making and

improvising music. His therapeutic journey has included changes in instruments (from the physical/rhythmic possibilities of the drum kit to the melodic character of the metallophone); changes in his experience of music (enhanced understanding of the nature of passive and active musical experiences); and changes in his experience of himself and of others.

Working with Peter highlights some fundamental differences between working with children and adults. Due to more than three score years of life experience, he can understand and articulate his experiences from the context of his long life. This makes his 'revelations' regarding his personal/musical experiences very enlightening, clarifying and confirming my understanding of his therapeutic journey. However, even with his ability to express himself verbally, he still struggles to describe his musical experiences and resorts to using global terms such as 'being heard, sharing, relaxation and expression'. For this reason, studying the tape recordings of his musical responses is a vital part of my work. Through listening both to his talking about his experiences and to the tapes, I can gain a more complete understanding of our joint therapeutic journey.

Within the music therapy context Peter has control and leads his own therapeutic journey. However, the journey is influenced by my role as a therapist and I make suggestions regarding musical styles, possibilities, instruments to use for our joint improvisations. Through the process of questioning, trial and error, give and take, our musical/therapeutic relationship develops. Apart from the time factor of an hour for the session, I allow as much freedom as possible to explore musical experiences. I tend to work alone with adults, since adults can feel inhibited about exploring unfamiliar mediums – particularly with active music-making. Should any significant issues arise during the session, which I think important to relay to nursing staff or other appropriate professionals, I always ask the client first for permission.

But back to the music!

Peter heads straight for the metallophone. From silence, he finds some exquisite gentle sounds on the pentatonic section of the instrument. I support this via simple two/three-note chords. The music develops with some characteristic motifs. It builds, climaxes and then subsides. It ends in silence. A held silence. This ending is new to us. A change has occurred. We move on – a new improvisation.

During the session we have a variety of musical experiences: shared musical ideas when the music flows between us effortlessly; moments when musically we seem to go off at tangents and our ideas are not connecting and moments when he musically teases me, to which I respond by engaging him in a musical race. Suddenly the hour is up. Peter can't believe it. The music has been vibrant and fulfilling for both of us. The experience and degree of contact within the music is the same as for Mary's session. An experience of a strong sense of ongoingness, energy and flow. A spiritual[4] connection has been made.

Later, while writing my notes on the session, I think about the paradox of music being based on time structures and yet giving an experience of timelessness.

3.00 p.m.

I have little time to recollect myself between Peter's session and Lucy's. The contrast could not be more extreme: from an experienced, worldly wise adult male who's been healthy for most of his life, to a tiny baby girl of ten months with a range of profound difficulties. I check with the Keech nurses to see if she's OK for a session. One HCA accompanies me.

Generally, when I'm working with the children, I have a member of the care team with me. This is for a variety of reasons, including education

4   I use the word 'spiritual' to describe, to the best of my ability, the experience that is elicited. Readers are encouraged to replace this with terms such as 'soul' or 'deep sense of awareness' etc. In using the term 'spirituality' I am not referring to any external deity or religious experience, although awareness of this experience may eventually lead on to this realisation.

regarding music therapy, any health-related concerns that may arise during the session, advice regarding the extent of movement/physical abilities and, given our litigious society, as means for protection against accusations of impropriety.

> Lucy is brought into the room in her buggy. I ask for her to be taken out and laid down on the blankets that I've already positioned on the floor for her. This gives her the opportunity for a less restricted experience while making it easier for me to present musical instruments etc.
>
> I turn on the video camera and we begin.

I use a more structured approach for children's sessions than for adult sessions. Partly influenced by my training background but also my personal experience as a therapist, I've found that children, especially young children, require a clear structure to relate to. If the structure is too loose or unclear they become unfocused and their attention slips. The level of musical relationship also declines. I employ the format of a starter song, the presentation of instruments and finally a closing song (beginning, middle and end!). Within these parameters I follow any responses that the children make, giving them the experience for control but still maintaining a secure safe environment with clear boundaries. This allows them to know where they are within the session. Another important consideration in the therapeutic journey for children is the therapist's need to be aware of the developmental aspects of childhood. Goals of therapy will usually be influenced by the need to support and/or stimulate particular developmental stages or new skills.

One of the most successful instruments in gaining initial responses with children of a similar level of ability as Lucy are the wind-chimes. Partly because of the sound quality (high, tingly sounds) but also because of the visual effect (bright and shiny), the chimes seem to draw the children into touching and then exploring the sounds.

As soon as I begin to sing 'hello', Lucy opens her eyes. There is no other response – no vocal sounds, no movement. I move around her from left to right and back again. This time she follows my movements. I attempt to encourage her to make vocal sounds by leaving gaps in the simple repeated melody of the song I've been using. No response. I've gained her attention but she's not moved into actively participating. I switch to using instruments.

Initially, Lucy doesn't respond. I persevere. Just when I'm beginning to think she's not going to respond, she makes a small twitch with her left hand. Is it a reflex or is she intentionally trying to touch the chimes? I continue offering the instrument. She reaches out and, with a sweeping motion, her tiny hand brushes past three or four chimes. She smiles. As a therapist, I'm pleased. In that small response she has given me clues as to the direction of the session, her level of awareness, her physical abilities and her levels of intention. As a person, I'm thrilled. Her smile lights up her whole face and in that moment I feel clearly the fullness of her 'Being'. I offer the instrument again and she responds again. While the chimes ring, I sing with and about the sounds she's making, highlighting the fact that they have been heard and acknowledged. She smiles again. A musical connection has been made. Then just as suddenly she stops, shuts her eyes and goes off to sleep. Even though she appears to be asleep I sing a soft 'good-bye' song. You never know how much is being heard, even when someone appears to be asleep or even unconscious!

The session has lasted for 15 minutes – quite long for a small child! The carer takes Lucy out again, happy at what she has witnessed.

What this emphasises to me is the immediacy of contact that is possible with young children. They have less developed barriers and defences than adults and are much more 'open' to receive. However, this also makes them very vulnerable. Accordingly, this places a great responsibility on the music therapist

Still musing over these thoughts I clear up the room and prepare myself for the last session of the day – Mike Jones on the IPU.

3.45 p.m.

Offering music for someone close to death and in a semi-conscious state is probably the most technically and emotionally demanding work that I do. For a family, being with a dying relative or loved one can be one of the most intimate moments in their relationship. Going into such a situation, I am especially careful not to intrude, and this demands a great level of awareness of the situation and sensitivity towards the family. Offering music at such a time can be very powerful and often brings forth tears. Music appears to go straight to the heart of people, breaking down barriers as it goes. This enables feelings to be expressed and shared and can aid the grieving process.

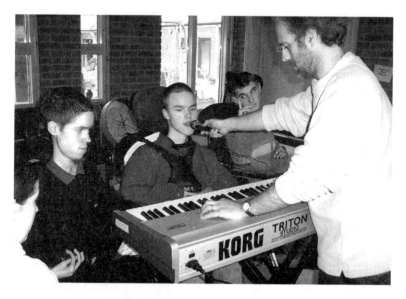

A recording session at Keech Cottage on a 'lads' weekend':
one of the musical activities which makes my work so varied

I knock on the door and Mrs Jones welcomes me in. The other family members have gone. Mike is moving his head from side to side and occasionally making vocal sounds. I set up the keyboard (new adaptor lead in tow!) and begin with a Bach prelude. As soon as I play, Mike stops his head movements and appears to listen. There is no way of knowing for certain whether he's aware of the music or not but his wife interprets it as listening and reaches out to him, sharing the moment. She draws closer to him, talking to him about the music. When I finish she recounts memories of the piece, for instance when he played it for their children. 'Do you remember?' she says to Mike. I play another piece; this time some gentle Chopin. Tears appear on Mrs Jones's face. She holds her husband's hand tightly. The music ends. There is silence for a few seconds and then Mrs Jones looks up. She smiles and says 'thank you'. She releases her husband's hand, stands up and approaches me. She looks right into my eyes, reaches out and we hug one another. Two total strangers, meeting through adversity, connecting through the experience of music. She thanks me once again and I leave. The session has only lasted 15 minutes. I report to the staff nurse in charge of the IPU, making her aware of events of the session. I go back to my office to write my notes.

The format of my notes is the same for both children and adults: observations, instruments/musical styles used, musical responses elicited and comments about the therapeutic process. There is a separate sheet for tape analysis. I think about the day. My overriding thoughts are focused in two areas. First, the experience of working with a medium that is so dominated by time structures but that gives an experience of timelessness. Second, that whether working with children or adults, the actual experience of making connections with people through music is the same.

Music can reach the depths of human experience. Music can also raise awareness of this human experience, which enables it to become shared.

Music highlights, I believe, the fact that we all share a common humanity regardless of our individual differences and prejudices.

Some weeks later Mrs Jones comes back to thank all the nurses who cared for her husband. She especially seeks me out and thanks me 'for making an otherwise unbearable situation more bearable'.

Chapter Nine

'This musical life': Tŷ Hafan Children's Hospice – a place for living

Diane Wilkinson

Tŷ Hafan opened in 1999 and I have been a part-time music therapist there since May 2000, when the hospice first received the support of Jessie's Fund. Indeed, the creation of the music therapy role at Tŷ Hafan was keenly awaited by many in South Wales, so I was particularly proud to be selected for it and feel privileged to be part of the many lives that have passed through the doors in that time.

I visit Tŷ Hafan one day each week for sessions with individual children, larger groups and families. Following an increase in funding, the hospice is now open seven days a week and provides respite, palliative and terminal care for children with life-limiting diseases and their families. Tŷ Hafan has a caring, supportive and relaxed atmosphere and creates a home-from-home experience, based on an individual and holistic approach which caters for the physical, emotional, social and spiritual needs of both the children and their families for as long as required. Set in beautiful grounds overlooking the sea, Tŷ Hafan is one of the UK's larger children's hospices, offering ten children's bedrooms as well as eight self-contained family rooms and a wealth of facilities including a sensory room, jacuzzi, music, computers and activity rooms and wonderful gardens.

Music in general, not just music therapy, plays a huge part in life at Tŷ Hafan. Day to day there is always a radio playing in the background and staff and care team members regularly use instruments to stimulate or relax the children in their care. From 'sing alongs' around the piano to organised concerts at Christmas, from jamming sessions in the lounge to services of Thanksgiving and Remembrance, life at Tŷ Hafan revolves around and is drawn together by song, sound and music, the importance of which is recognised and appreciated by all. As such, my role there is multifaceted: music therapist, musician and group facilitator, as well as team member and friend.

The musical life of which I write is such an intrinsic and powerful force at Tŷ Hafan that it would be impossible to think of the place without it. When I walk into Tŷ Hafan each week, I am never greeted by silence; rather, by a cacophony of sound and music. From the happy babble of everyday life to the poignancy of a reflective flute piece in the Memorial Garden, music touches each and every visitor to Tŷ Hafan and offers them a unique and personal experience.

The Tŷ Hafan Garden of Remembrance

The Christmas concert

Christmas is long anticipated by all children and those at Tŷ Hafan are no exception. In fact quite the opposite is true, as the end of November sees the start of frantic rehearsals for the annual pantomime, weekly servings of Christmas fayre and preparations for a concert for staff, families, children and visitors which usually takes place during the last week before the Christmas break. For this I work with staff and activity co-ordinators to devise a short service or concert which is interactive and as lively as possible. It gives everyone a chance to sing, play and laugh together in celebration. Although the concert celebrates the Christmas season, its aim is to be inclusive and multi-faith. The emphasis is on having fun, which never seems to be too difficult at Tŷ Hafan.

The concert comprises well-known and loved carols, jokes, poems, readings and an interactive talk, during which everyone is encouraged to join in with songs, sound effects, conjuring and games, all of which contribute to his unique telling of a particular Christmas story. Traditionally, the concert takes place with everyone in a good mood, having eaten their fill of one of Dave the Chef's fabulous Christmas dinners.

Music seems to offer children a new level of awareness and as families and visitors alike become aware of the smiles, vocal sounds and expressions of pleasure and satisfaction on the faces of their children (sometimes a rare or unusual sight), they are spurred on to lose their own inhibitions and to really enjoy themselves. Staff and care team members also take their lead from the children and demonstrate an openness and warmth which contributes to creating a cherished memory for all those involved.

The need to make the most of every celebration and the positive feeling of hope for a new year seems all the more important. The very genuine willingness of all those involved to embrace the joy and fun of the moment is touching and strengthening. Voices raised in song have a powerful way of bringing us all together, making us become one and focusing our thoughts on the important things in life: living, togetherness and collecting memories. The Christmas concert at Tŷ Hafan provides a bonding experience, derived from a sense of community and sharing, as people of all faiths, beliefs and upbringings come together to wish each other well for the festive season.

A time for relaxation

Working at Tŷ Hafan has its own anxieties and pressures, and there are occasions when times are difficult, tiring or frustrating. Times of many losses or perhaps a week where many individual children struggle to gel as a group can leave staff feeling somewhat isolated from each other and the group as a whole. Such times highlight the need for togetherness and unity, when the strong bond between team workers, usually so evident at Tŷ Hafan, needs a little support and sustenance. On such occasions, a session of restful music can afford both staff and the children in their care a time of relaxation, peaceful communication and self-expression. I include an extract from clinical notes which detail one such session. Of course, names have been changed.

> Gina, Vicky, Anna, Jack and Tania enjoy a relaxation session in the sensory room. We play for about 45 minutes, mostly flute, although I bring in the ocean drum, bells, maracas and cabasa. The flute is interspersed with periods of easy quiet and, towards the end of the time, laughter and clapping. Each of the children responds differently. Gina is very quiet all the way through, engrossed with a wooden box. Vicky is much more active, shouting and laughing from time to time and exploring any instrument she can find. Anna moves around constantly, vocalising to the sound of the flute, crawling over to me at one point and grabbing the instrument in an attempt to blow it herself. After a couple of attempts she pushes it back to me and indicates that I should start again, smiling as I do so. She seems quite a character. Jack is very relaxed indeed, as is Tania; they both vocalise gently…

The children gradually begin to co-operate musically as a collective, rather than a group of individuals. The pitch of their vocal sounds becomes closer to each other and begins to evolve as an accompaniment for my flute-playing, each contributing an important aspect of the impro-vised music as a whole. Staff remain mostly quiet at first but begin to express themselves more freely during the later stages of the session.

More often than not, the sessions with these particular children are on a one-to-one basis – but this spontaneous and informal group session provides an opportunity for both the care team and the children to create a bond, on which they are able to draw for comfort and safety. The atmosphere becomes more positive in the hours which follow. Facilitating such bonding is one of the many ways in which music positively influences life at Tŷ Hafan and being the facilitator is one of the joys of working with music at the hospice.

A service of Thanksgiving and Remembrance

Each summer, Tŷ Hafan welcomes back bereaved families for a service of Thanksgiving and Remembrance. This is an open and inclusive gathering with no particular religious inclination, although it retains a spiritual basis which encourages and gives support to expressions of grief, reflection and the celebration of life. The service takes place in the hospice grounds in a marquee, which provides a sense of occasion while maintaining a certain detachment from the life that families remember at Tŷ Hafan.

Finding comfort in familiar surroundings, words and music, the bereaved families are encouraged to join in a sense of shared experience as well as to take time for themselves to remember as they choose. There are flowers everywhere and families are free to wander around the hospice and gardens both before and after the service. Tears and laughter are equally in evidence and, indeed, equally valid. Families clearly derive real comfort from meeting up with friends made during their child's visits and from the knowledge that others have also experienced their very particular loss and pain, grieving and healing.

The service is simple, sincere and poignant, beginning with a welcome which emphasises Tŷ Hafan's continuing support for families. A hymn then follows, traditionally 'Make me a channel of your peace', and then candles are lit for the children who have died, for those present and for those unable to attend. Prayers are also said for the families, parents, grandparents and siblings as well as for hospice staff and friends.

Make me a channel of your peace

Make me a channel of your peace.
Where there is hatred let me bring your love;
Where there is injury, your pardon Lord:
And where there's doubt, true faith in you.

Oh Master, grant that I may never seek
So much to be consoled as to console;
To be understood as to understand
To be loved, as to love with all my soul.

Make me a channel of your peace.
Where there's despair in life let me bring hope;
Where there is darkness, only light;
And where there's sadness, ever joy.

Make me a channel of your peace.
It is in pardoning that we are pardoned,
In giving to all men that we receive;
And in dying that we are born to eternal life.

St Francis, quoted in Dominica 1997

During the lighting of candles, reflective music is played, Fauré or
Debussy for example, both to give time and significance to the candle
lighting and to provide an atmosphere of quiet reflection and calmness.
The staff present (one for each family) are encouraged to show their
feelings as well as care for the families during the day. For me, it is
important to have the sheet music in front of me, to enable me to keep the
slightly detached perspective which I find necessary as a performer.
Being integrally involved with many of the children remembered, I
would otherwise find it impossible not to be moved by the occasion,
making it difficult to perform the important role entrusted to me during
the service.

My overriding feeling is that it is an *important* event and that, whereas
my music provides a certain atmosphere and elicits a certain response
from those hearing it, it remains a tool and a feature of the service as a

whole, allowing families to appreciate their own personal and unique experience of the occasion. That said, it is impossible to ignore the music's powerful effect on those present; how it can serve as a trigger for emotion, as well as a comfort, and a tribute for those who have died.

Readings from inspiring poems, popular songs or extracts from books, and an address by the Director of Care, form the next section of the service, followed by the second song, 'Fleetingly Known Yet Ever Remembered', sung to the tune of 'Morning Has Broken'.

Fleetingly known, yet ever remembered

Fleetingly known, yet ever remembered,
These are our children now and always:
These whom we see not we will forget not,
Morning and evening all of our days.

Lives that touched our lives, tenderly, briefly,
Now in the one light living always:
Names in our hearts now, safe from all harm now,
We will remember all of our days.

As we recall them, silently name them,
Open our hearts, Lord, now and always:
Grant to us, grieving, love for the living;
Strength for each other all of our days.

Safe in your peace Lord, hold these our children;
Grace, light and laughter grant them each day:
Cherish and hold them till we may know them
When to your glory we find our way.

Christina Rossetti, quoted in Dominica 1997

The group then moves to the Garden of Remembrance, a special place in the hospice grounds with a stream as its central feature. Here each family is presented with a pebble engraved with the name of their child, which they are invited to place amongst those already there, in the stream. Symbolically, over time, the names fade along with the pain of loss, while the pebbles and the treasured memories of their loved ones always remain.

This final section of the service, again accompanied by reflective music, allows families to linger by the garden or to move away as they choose, without the definite silence of the end of an occasion which can sometimes be awkward.

On reflection

The effect of the songs and music played at this service are perhaps the most poignant example of how music is important at Tŷ Hafan. 'This musical life' is a powerful force of its own. Without it, we face a hollow and pale substitute for the vibrant, colourful existence of which we are all capable. Without it, we face a barrier to the unique and personal experience which music can provide in this precious gift of life.

Reference

Dominica, F. (1997) *Just My Reflection – Helping Parents To Do Things Their Way When Their Child Dies.* London: Darton Longman and Todd.

Chapter Ten

From hospice to home:
Music therapy outreach

Kathryn Nall and Elinor Everitt

This chapter describes the setting up and running of a project, the Music Therapy Home Visiting Service (referred to simply as 'the project'), which takes music therapy directly into children's homes. The chapter describes the benefits of music therapy both for children with life-limiting conditions and their families in the home environment.

Music therapy was in the early stages of development at this particular children's hospice when Kathryn Nall took over as the music therapist. At that time all the music therapy took place in the hospice itself, and there was a clear need for music therapists to travel into different counties, to take the service into children's homes.

Elinor Everitt was one of the first music therapists recruited into the project, and she shares some examples of her work to illustrate the project's unique benefits.

Kathryn's vision

Although music therapy had only been established within the hospice for a very short time, it had already proved its value to the children who used its facilities for both respite and palliative care. Staff and management had been impressed by the way music therapy provided a vital means of communication and self-expression for children with life-limiting conditions for whom verbal communication was difficult or impossible. However, the impact music therapy could make was limited, there being only six hours available for music therapy during the week.

Taking music therapy into the family home had been an idea of Kathryn's predecessor Vicky Kenny, who had identified some children who could benefit from longer periods of music therapy than was possible during their stays of respite care. Many of these children were unable to access other sources of music therapy, either because it was unavailable or because they were too frail to attend a school or centre. The very wide geographical area served by the hospice meant that visiting the children in their own homes would be very time-consuming, and there were insufficient hours for the hospice music therapist to do this. Together with Lesley Schatzberger, development director of Jessie's Fund, Kathryn put together a proposal for the management and trustees of both the hospice and Jessie's Fund.

This proposal outlined a vision for a service that could provide music therapy at home for a limited number of children, with Jessie's Fund contributing half of the funding, providing the hospice would make up the rest. In order to be cost-effective, Kathryn proposed that music therapists for the project be recruited to take on individual pieces of work for up to 16 weeks. As hospice music therapist, Kathryn would be the project co-ordinator and oversee its setting up and development. Stephanie's story illustrated to the hospice how music therapy in the home can meet the identified needs for children with life-limiting conditions.

Stephanie: Music therapy with a housebound teenager

Stephanie was a normal active child until she reached the age of nine, when she developed a progressive and degenerative condition which has left her unable to access or participate in any normal school activities. Music therapy is the only remaining service identified on Stephanie's statement of special needs from which she can benefit. Stephanie has not been able to attend school for several years as travel is difficult and uncomfortable for her, so all medical and educational input is received at home. She learnt an instrument as a child and continues to show a love of music. Stephanie is now unable to perform even the simplest movement for herself and has no speech.

Stephanie particularly responds to songs that she knows well, for example 'Loch Lomond', 'My Bonny Lies Over the Ocean', 'An English Country Garden' and 'Greensleeves'. I use songs (not necessarily with their words) that reflect Stephanie's current mood and her more able past, through a mix of major and minor harmonies. Using songs that Stephanie recognises enables her to vocalise with me, and often leads into improvisation and musical conversation where we take turns to sing or play. Sometimes Stephanie finds it difficult to create the sound she wants to sing, but when she does her face lights up with a beaming smile and she shows increased levels of alertness.

Music therapy has become a very special time for Stephanie, where her feelings and preferences can be attended to away from the time-consuming tasks of daily care. Her mother also values this brief time when they can be apart in the house, commenting that 'music therapy is the one thing that she can do independently; it is an important part of her week'. Music therapy also provides Stephanie with some control, where she can interact with another person through her vocalisation. She clearly enjoys using her voice and communicating with those around her. The music provides a clear structure, and also the freedom to express something of herself and how she is feeling. None of this could happen if the music therapist were unable to offer sessions in Stephanie's home.

Setting up the project

The trustees of both charities agreed to setting up the project for an initial one-year period. Joint funding was to be sufficient for ten children to receive up to 16 music therapy sessions each in their own homes. As project co-ordinator, Kathryn was to provide a detailed evaluation report to the trustees at the end of the year. Kathryn needed to spend some time recruiting music therapists for this very different way of working, and soon established a core team of therapists prepared to commit to at least one piece of work. All the therapists were state registered and police-checked by the Criminal Records Bureau prior to starting the work.

In setting up a project within the unique setting of children's family homes, there are a lot of important professional and practical implications to take into account before the work can start.

Professional issues

It is essential for therapists to have a working knowledge of child protection issues. Communication and liaison with the families and the hospice is vital to the success of this home-based work, but this can be difficult to achieve as hospice staff work on a shift system with variable hours. To help address this problem Kathryn set up a system of recording acceptable to both families and staff. This helps to sustain relationships of confidentiality and trust with all those concerned in the care and welfare of the children. Channels of communication need to be kept open with schools, and also with health and social service professionals, in order to avoid overloading families with too many services at any one time.

One of the key tasks of the project co-ordinator is to make regular contact with the therapists and to be available to discuss any problems or concerns, and Kathryn became increasingly aware of the need to ensure that the therapists had access to appropriate support and supervision when working in isolated environments. Although all the therapists were having their own external supervision, they lacked opportunities to meet together and share with others doing similar work. Kathryn set up a peer support group for all project therapists, which meets on a regular basis.

Practical implications

When a hospice serves a very wide geographical area there are inevitably logistical problems; for example, in the use of the therapist's time and travel and the availability of therapists and suitable instruments. Travel costs were reduced by recruiting music therapists within the different geographical areas. After the first year it was acknowledged that the work had been taking up more time than the hour that had originally been allocated to each session, and the trustees agreed that the time allocated to each session could be increased and used flexibly.

The children

Kathryn and the hospice staff prioritised referrals by considering the complexity of the children's needs and their responsiveness to music. During its first year, the project relied mainly on the knowledge of the hospice staff for referrals, so as not to raise families' expectations until evaluations were completed.

Parents of sick children can feel angry or guilty when coming to terms with their loss of expectations for a healthy child. Also, the sheer physical effort and anxiety surrounding the child's care can leave little time for parents to just 'be' with their child, getting to know him or her and having fun together. The music therapist can support the bond between parent and child by supporting any interactions that take place, and giving parents or carers ideas for using music creatively with their child as a positive way of being together. The next two stories, of Shelina and Ollie, show how two children with very different needs, as well as their families, can benefit from music therapy in the home.

Shelina: Working with a child and her mother

Shelina is two and a half, and, at the time, was an only child. Shelina has birth asphyxia resulting in severe developmental delay, cortical blindness and feeding problems. The severity of Shelina's disabilities means that she is very limited in what she can do, even with support.

In music therapy I use a tactile approach, allowing Shelina plenty of time to explore the instruments through touch. I gently brush a Peruvian seed rattle across her hands and legs, or I play a drum while Shelina's mother holds her hands on the drum to feel the vibrations.

Music therapy is used to support and encourage the development of Shelina's sounds or movements. Songs are important in our work. They provide a clear structure, and also enable us to work flexibly. We sing the tune of 'Daddy's Taking Us to the Zoo Tomorrow' to sing about 'Shelina's Bouncing on Mummy's

Knee', or I might use two differently pitched chime bars to reflect Shelina being swayed from side to side by her mother. Shelina has developed the use of a distinctive sound to ask for a song to be repeated, which enables her to take some control over what we do in the sessions.

Music therapy came at an important time for Shelina and her mother in the development of their relationship. We talked about suggestions made by the different professionals who visited the family, and thought about how music might help Shelina to understand her daily routine. In particular, we developed songs to support the physiotherapy exercises that Shelina did with her mother each day. By using well-known songs and changing the words as appropriate, I provided Shelina's mother with a new repertoire of songs and a means to explore making up her own songs with Shelina.

When music therapy takes place at home, family members participate sometimes on a very *ad hoc* basis, depending on who is present on that day (and with no advance preparation!). This inclusive approach – not unfamiliar to hospice music therapists – enables families to share special times together to alleviate and accompany other 'caring' tasks, such as physiotherapy, or to support fragile or developing relationships.

Ollie: Working with siblings

As project co-ordinator, Kathryn felt it important that siblings should not feel left out of this project, since siblings of children with life-limiting conditions may have complex feelings that include anger, jealousy or guilt at being healthy. They may feel that they are in some way responsible for their sibling's illness, and may feel neglected because of all the time and attention needed by the 'sick' child. These feelings may show themselves in difficult behaviours, such as aggression, defiance or poor sleep patterns. There may also be unspoken fears that they too may become ill and die, or that they might lose their parents and be left with the care of their brother or sister.

Ollie is almost two, the younger of two boys. As a baby Ollie had 18 heart operations in 14 months and frequent subsequent hospital admissions. As a result of his multiple heart, lung and feeding problems, his life has been dominated by his medical needs: he is on oxygen 24 hours a day, making travel difficult.

Ollie and his brother Edward received 34 music therapy sessions over a period of 61 weeks. This was unusual for the project, but hospice staff felt that music therapy was so vital that they secured extra funds from another source for it to continue for as long as possible.

Whenever I arrive at Ollie's home, he sees my blue box of musical instruments and immediately becomes very animated, smiling and moving his arms as he anticipates the music to come. Ollie enjoys choosing and playing the different instruments and plays the drums vigorously using big arm movements. The contrast between Ollie's playing and the delicacy of his medical condition remains striking. Vocalising has played an increasingly important part in my sessions with Ollie, and I have been encouraged by his developing speech and eye contact.

I use children's songs and musical games with Ollie and Edward to encourage turn-taking and sharing. Gradually, the brothers have become more accepting of each other's ideas, taking it in turns to choose an activity or instruments for one another. We use songs such as 'I am a Music Man' to provide each of us with the chance to play a solo and for us all to play together. Edward's love of dancing encourages Ollie to develop his movements, as he sits on the floor and watches his brother dance.

Music therapy provided Ollie with the opportunity to take some control and make choices about what we did in the sessions. This was in contrast to the prescribed medical routine of Ollie's life. I was unusual in being a non-medical professional who visited the home and did not have to carry out unpleasant procedures. When I began my visits, Ollie's mother commented: 'You are the only person who does not have to prod and poke him.' The boys' mother was not involved in music therapy, and the sessions provided her with time for herself.

Ollie's frequent emergency hospital admissions restricted what the family could do together. In music therapy Ollie and Edward could share a special time playing and being together as equals, and this went some way to addressing their sibling rivalry.

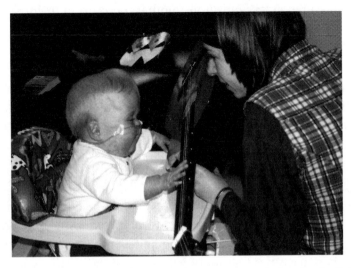

Ollie strums the guitar and increasingly vocalises with Elinor during their 'Hello' song

The project develops

After a successful review at the end of the first year, financial support was granted for a further two years from both Jessie's Fund and the hospice. A significant development in the project was the extension of the work with a dying child and pre-bereaved siblings to further work with siblings post-bereavement. An example of this work is illustrated in Jessica's story.

Jessica: Music therapy with a terminally ill child and her siblings

Jessica was 11 years old and the oldest of three daughters. She was referred for music therapy during the last stages of a degenerative condition, which resulted in very poor hearing, blindness, immobility and pain. Although Jessica was in the terminal stage of her illness, she attended school on a part-time basis when she could. However, she received music therapy at home. This enabled me to provide music therapy for Jessica on a regular basis in the most appropriate way, depending on how she was feeling, whether lying on her bed or sitting in her wheelchair. Music was always a great love of Jessica's and a suitable medium for her to express herself and to have some enjoyment and relaxation as her condition deteriorated. We had nine sessions before she died.

In our sessions I used songs that were particular favourites from Jessica's early years: 'She'll be Coming Round the Mountain' had become a way of engaging her and reflecting on her more able past life. Jessica responded to the music with wide-open eyes, moving instruments, especially the tambourine, between her hands, playing the guitar with me and often relaxing, showing her enjoyment of the music.

On two occasions I worked with her sisters, Hollie and Annie, while Jessica is in respite care. We took turns to play and listen to each other, and they enjoyed singing me some of their favourite songs. By working with Hollie and Annie as well as with Jessica, I came to recognise all of their needs for special times to be themselves and reflect on their changing family circumstances.

After Jessica's death, and because they've enjoyed the music so much, Hollie and Annie received joint music therapy sessions at school to support them in their bereavement. Songs continue to be an important part of the work. We made a tape of songs that remind Hollie and Annie of Jessica, and also made up our own song, 'If You Knew Jessie', which helped us to share our memories.

Our last story in this chapter, concerning Jessie, illustrates a transferring of music therapy in the 'other' direction: from home to school – where the music therapist works closely with the school staff to support and address a child's educational needs.

Jessie: Music therapy from home to school

Jessie is aged six and the second child of a single-parent family. Jessie's severe and complex medical condition can change rapidly, requiring continuous nursing care. As this nursing care is not available at school Jessie is unable to attend for a prolonged period. The ability to meet Jessie's developmental and social needs at home was limited to what her mother could give her, so she was referred for music therapy. Jessie received her first few music therapy sessions at home, where the development of our strong therapeutic relationship enabled a smooth transfer of her music therapy to school. Although the physical space changed with the transfer, our session content remained consistent.

At school I work with Jessie's nurse and support worker, and we discuss ways in which music can be used to work towards her educational aims. For example, music is used to develop the use of her physically weaker left side, by encouraging Jessie to reach out and play the guitar and keyboard in particular. I also play short sharp sounds, for example on a wood block, to encourage Jessie to turn to where the sound is coming from to develop her awareness of her surroundings.

To provide continuity in the work with Jessie, I provide her support team with some basic musical ideas to use with her, while the school investigates providing music therapy themselves. The staff ask for a song to accompany cleaning Jessie's teeth, so we write new words to a familiar tune. I also suggest ways of using familiar children's songs, adapting them to encourage different movements and looking skills. In particular I encourage the staff to enjoy vocalising and babbling freely with Jessie, taking turns to sing and imitating each other's sounds and mouth shapes.

Evaluation of the project

At the end of each year of the project Kathryn writes a report evaluating the progress and outcomes of this home-based music therapy approach, and this report shows that regular music therapy within the home setting makes a significant contribution to meeting the needs of children with a life-limiting condition.

One of the benefits is that music therapy is a non-medical intervention and is anticipated with pleasure by sick children at home, as illustrated by Ollie. For some families, there is the unexpected relief of having a half hour off for a cup of tea while their child has exclusive time of therapy: in other words, music therapy sessions provide a time for healthy separation, as expressed by Stephanie's mother. For others, music therapy at home means creative time shared by family members. Also, family time away from the stress of routine care tasks helps to support and develop relationships, often facilitating interactions in ways that are new. For a few, such as Shelina and her mother, it is helpful to give parents or carers ideas and guidance for sharing music together aside from music therapy sessions.

For the children themselves there are the more established benefits of regular music therapy. These include opportunities for children to experience choice and control, the space to express difficult feelings, the opportunity to improve the quality of sibling relationships (for Ollie and Edward), a release from pain (for Jessica), or a time of relaxation that can enable a child to become more receptive to other therapies (such as physiotherapy for Shelina).

Although the majority of Jessie's music therapy took place at school, the sessions first took place at home, providing valuable physical stimulation, social interaction and a place for her to express herself. Jessie's love of music and her animated response led to the development of a strong therapeutic relationship, through which the transition to school was eased. For some of the children in the project, providing music therapy at home encouraged families to investigate setting up music therapy at school. In providing this encouragement, the project opened up opportunities that had never before been realised and could not have been achieved by the hospice alone.

Siblings' complicated feelings aroused by loss can result in their premature acceptance of responsibilities, and sometimes an ambition to help other children with a similar condition. These feelings need time to be explored and understood if they are not to linger as unresolved feelings of guilt or anger (Sutton 2002). Even quite small children can feel this need to take responsibility for others, as experienced by one of the project music therapists working with the three-year-old brother of a terminally ill child. This little boy pretended to make a huge chocolate cake with all the musical instruments, for 'everyone in the world', perhaps to make them feel better.

Bereaved siblings may have spiritual issues and questions that need to be addressed. One little girl explored this through the notion of angels, and after just three sessions she asked the therapist 'I wonder what music the angels are playing now in heaven?', perhaps her way of asking where her sister was now and what she might be doing.

Unless these experiences and feelings find an outlet or are explored in some way they are likely to be intensified in the future. Music therapy is one way of helping to deal with these feelings, as described in Chapter 4 of this book. The hospice has a strong family support team that includes specialist workers for siblings, and they arrange appropriate work or events for these children either individually or in groups. As the project has developed, the hospice staff have begun to refer siblings whom they feel could be helped to communicate and express themselves best through music therapy.

The project continues. Our vision is becoming a reality, with music therapy moving outwards from the hospice, beginning to reach into the homes of those children who are most in need of the creative and therapeutic power of music.

Note

At the request of all of the families, the children's names have been retained.

Reference

Sutton, J. (ed.) (2002) *Music, Music Therapy, and Trauma – International Perspectives.* London: Jessica Kingsley Publishers.

Chapter Eleven

Needing support:
A therapist's perspective

Gill Cubitt

I began working part-time in a small children's hospice in rural Norfolk shortly after qualifying as a music therapist in 2000. Before training, I had worked for many years as a music teacher. Starting work in a children's hospice felt challenging; it was different to anything that the training course could have prepared me for. Like many newly qualified music therapists, I was keen to put into practice what I had learned in the training course, but was dismayed to find that aspects of my therapeutic persona needed some rethinking to work in a hospice setting. I needed to find my own way of working, but also needed some support from other music therapists working in a similar setting and from my hospice colleagues.

This chapter explores the themes of feeling new, and finding support, through a fictional character, Viola Truenote. Through several fictional episodes I observe Viola's early weeks at work in a children's hospice. Each episode is followed by my own reflections on her situation.

★

Using storytelling, and in particular the language of a children's story, allows me, as the writer, to present difficult feelings and experiences in an accessible and entertaining way. In this book, which is about work with children, the language of a children's story feels particularly appropriate.

Stories, like therapy, can work on many different levels. Since humour is an important ingredient in a children's hospice, it feels right to use gentle humour here. After all, the main object of amusement is our heroine, Viola, as she struggles to find her own way of working in a situation quite unlike anything she has experienced during her music therapy training. Like Viola, I needed to learn that being a therapist is something that I had to grow into. Outward signs such as Viola's 'hats and badges' (or the theoretical orientation of a training course) are less important than personal qualities such as warmth, empathy, the ability to be flexible and, perhaps most importantly, the ability to laugh at one's own mistakes.

The children described are all composite children, based on many different children I have worked with over the last three years. Such artistic licence allows me to write more freely.

Let's meet Viola, as she arrives at the children's hospice for her first day at work...

In which Viola begins work

One hot summer's day, in a time and universe quite similar to this, the children and staff at Snowdrops Children's Hospice were momentarily distracted from their morning routine by the insistent ringing of the doorbell. Mary, one of the nurses, opened the door. She was greeted by a woman of uncertain age, wearing a large blue straw hat out of which poked long tendrils of red straggly hair. The hat was emblazoned with the words 'Acme Academy of Music Therapy'. The woman looked rather hot and flustered; strands of long red hair escaped from underneath the hat, and she was breathing rapidly. On her sweatshirt was pinned a large green badge, which claimed that the wearer was Viola Truenote from the Guild of Music Therapists.

'You'd better come in,' said Mary, rather doubtfully. 'We're expecting you.'

'That's a strange hat,' exclaimed a small, red-faced boy spinning around in a red wheelchair. 'Are you in fancy dress?'

'No,' said Viola, feeling rather foolish. 'It's my music therapist's hat; we're supposed to wear it all the time.'

Viola had only just received the hat and badge on graduating from the Academy in Metropolisville. She had been looking forward to wearing them, and had seen lots of music therapists in their hats and badges in the big city. However, in the small children's hospice in rural Angleshire, which was to be her first music therapy post, hats and badges seemed rather out of place.

'Can I borrow it?' asked the small boy. 'I'm going to play with the rabbit in a bit; perhaps he could sit inside it!'

The experience of feeling new is not unusual: starting at a new school, beginning a course at college, and starting work are common events in many people's lives. However, starting work as a music therapist in a children's hospice feels a bit like being thrown in at the deep end! There is no fixed routine, there may be different children staying at hospice each week, and they will have a wide range of medical conditions. Some children, like the small boy in the red wheelchair, can talk and are fairly mobile, but others may never have acquired the use of spoken language or may have more restricted movement. Some degree of sensory impairment may need to be taken into account as well. Many children have some degree of learning disability, often coupled with complex medical needs. The staff who care for the children are a mixture of nurses and carers, all of whom work shifts. No wonder Viola feels a bit anxious on her first day! Trying to work out how to introduce music therapy into such a complex environment can feel rather daunting!

Viola comes with various expectations and anxieties of her own, which could lead her into difficulties. She is keen to tell everyone all about music therapy, but in her somewhat evangelistic fervour she forgets that perhaps not everyone wants to know. Like all music therapists trained in the UK, Viola has done a recognised training course which qualifies her to work as a music therapist. Each training course has a different theoretical orientation: hence Viola's badge, which she is very proud to wear, and her hat, which looks like fancy dress to the boy in the wheelchair. He knows nothing about music therapy and rapidly brings Viola down to earth with his honest comments! Of course, in the real world music therapists don't wear fancy hats or badges. However, remaining true to one's training while being brave enough to adapt to a new working environment can be a real challenge to any music therapist starting work. The ever-changing environment of a children's hospice may be particularly challenging.

Let's return to Viola the following week…

In which Viola finds a friend

Viola was feeling pleased with herself. She had sorted out the instrument cupboard in Snowdrops Hospice, met various nurses and carers and now she was visiting Daisy House, a small children's hospice on the outskirts of Rivertown. Viola hadn't begun any music therapy sessions yet; she had come to visit Gloria Clearvoice, the music therapist at Daisy House, as part of her induction period. She rang the bell and was shown into a modern, purpose-built building. Gloria came to meet her. She had short fair hair and was dressed in a pink T-shirt and jeans; there was no sign of any hat or badge. (Viola made a mental note to ask her about this at a later date.)

After coffee and a bit of a chat, Gloria asked Viola if she would like to act as her assistant that morning. Viola eagerly agreed, and went to fetch her violin from the car. They worked with two girls, one after another. Jenny had her session first. She was around ten years old, with a severe form of cerebral palsy and associated medical problems. Jenny had no movement in her lower body, but some restricted movement in her hands. She was non-verbal, but Gloria knew that Jenny had a good understanding of spoken language. Viola tried to follow Gloria's lead, playing a harmony line on her violin when it seemed appropriate, holding an ocean drum for Jenny to explore and, later, helping her to feel the strings of a small harp. Gloria used the guitar, piano and voice. She had worked with Jenny before, so she had found out which sounds might attract her, and whether there were any particular songs that Jenny might like to hear. Jenny seemed tense at the beginning of the session; her vocalising had a sharp edge to it. However, by the end of the session, which lasted for around half an hour, Jenny looked more relaxed and her vocalising had a more playful and gentle quality. The session ended with a good-bye song. There was a brief pause while Gloria and Viola tidied the room and got ready for Cheryl, who was loudly telling everyone that she was going to play the drum kit.

Cheryl was 16, with Down's syndrome and serious heart problems. Cheryl walked confidently into the room asking Gloria to 'Play some pop!' which Gloria did on the piano, while Cheryl hit the snare and hi-hat very loudly, maintaining a regular beat. Viola felt unsure of how best to assist in this session, but eventually settled on playing a contrasting rhythm on a small djembe (a drum). This session was a bit longer and ended with Cheryl drumming to a rock-style good-bye, Gloria playing the piano and Viola playing on the violin. After both sessions there was time for Viola and Gloria to talk about each of the sessions before Gloria wrote up the clinical notes in each child's file. Viola felt encouraged after these sessions and was very glad that Gloria had asked her to help. There was a lot for her to think about as she drove back to Snowdrops in the car, and she felt excited at the thought of beginning her own sessions the following week.

★

Viola is beginning to realise that she can learn a lot from other music therapists who work in similar situations. As Viola has only recently qualified, her experience of music therapy with children is limited to those with whom she worked as part of her training course. She may not have worked with children with severe learning disabilities, so meeting Gloria and acting as her assistant is a helpful introduction to this work, as it gives Viola some ideas which she can adapt to her own situation. Many music therapists working in children's hospices can feel isolated, as they may be the only one in their particular hospice. Meeting up with another music therapist and observing some of their sessions can reduce that sense of isolation and provide much-needed support and advice. Viola is still rather hung up on outward signs such as hats and badges, but she is not too proud to accept help, even when she isn't sure of Gloria's theoretical orientation! She is also beginning to learn that she can provide support herself, by acting as Gloria's co-therapist and by sharing her thoughts about each of the sessions. Perhaps Viola is also beginning to realise that working alongside a music therapist who has done a different training course can be beneficial, offering a different perspective and another way of working.

Let's return to Viola, who is now back at Snowdrops, about to have her first musical encounter...

In which a parcel arrives and music therapy sessions begin

Viola was in the music room, getting out a selection of instruments. She was going to begin music therapy sessions that very morning and felt excited, nervous and uncertain how to begin. She noticed a large package, perched on top of a cupboard, and lifted it down. It was addressed to her. Perhaps it was the drum that she had ordered last week? At that moment, she became aware that someone was watching her.

'Hello,' said a small voice from behind the open door.

'Hello,' replied Viola as she began unwrapping the parcel. A small girl aged about three, with long blonde hair and wearing a denim dress and pink trainers, peeped around the door.

'What's that?' asked the girl as she skipped into the room.

'I don't know!' exclaimed Viola. 'Why don't you help me open it?'

Viola and the small girl (whose name was Alice) opened the box together. The box was bigger than Alice, and eventually opened to reveal a large drum, with a skin top and shiny silver sides.

'Oh, can I try it?' exclaimed Alice in wonder. Viola agreed, and found a chair for Alice to stand on. Viola offered to close the door, but Alice said that she wouldn't be staying for long, as she wanted to do some painting next. Alice began to beat the drum with her hands, laughing at its deep sound, while Viola tried to find a way of responding, using low chords on the piano and her voice. After a few minutes, Alice stopped playing and jumped down from her chair.

'I've finished now,' she announced, and ran out.

Many children who visit the hospice for respite have no idea what a music therapy session means, and are often very curious about the instruments, or about the therapist. They may come in to 'test the waters' rather like Alice, before deciding that music therapy might be OK. Viola had left the door open while she was getting ready, and had she not done so, Alice might never have wandered in and the encounter might never have taken place. Often, such casual encounters may pave the way for more substantial sessions, which might take place weeks or even months later.

I'll leave this episode about Alice with a question: is Viola's ten-minute encounter with a small girl unwrapping a drum and then playing it her first music therapy session in the hospice? I like to think so, but leave you, as reader, to decide…

Let's catch up with Viola, fast-forwarding now to around six months after she began to work. Viola has just encountered her first death since she began work…

In which everyone says good-bye to Peter

Viola sat down in the nurses' station. Tears ran silently down her face. She had just been into see Peter for the last time. He had looked so small, lying there in bed with his long dark fringe falling over his eyes and his mouth slightly open. His skin was a bit grey. This had surprised Viola, but otherwise Peter looked fine, tucked into his favourite woollen blanket. Peter had died earlier that day and his small body had been brought to the hospice by his parents. Viola was glad that she had been able to see him, to say good-bye.

'Are you all right?' asked Sonia, one of the nurses. Viola nodded, not feeling brave enough to speak. 'Would you like a cup of tea?' asked Sonia. Again, Viola nodded. She wished she didn't cry quite so easily, but this didn't matter right now. Sonia went off to make the tea, and Viola blew her nose noisily, glancing out of the window. Outside, the daffodils waved their heads jauntily and the sun shone, but inside everything felt cold and grey because, for one small child, everything was over.

★

It's not always easy to predict the impact of a particular child's death. Perhaps Viola has become particularly close to Peter during their time together at the hospice, or perhaps she has felt more emotionally involved because Peter is the first child she has seen after death.

Although this episode is fictional it is based on real experiences, and writing this section has felt particularly challenging for me. Some of you may be surprised to know that a child's body might come to the hospice: this seems to be becoming more common. Parents may prefer to bring their child's body to the hospice for a few days, rather than send it to an undertaker, which can seem a bit impersonal. Having the body at the hospice also enables staff to say good-bye, and can help each person to come to terms with what has happened.

Viola hasn't seen a child's body before, and she finds herself overcome with emotion. However, she's come a long way since her first day at work in the hospice and is now able to share her feelings more openly. Viola's growing trust in her colleagues means that they now feel able to offer her some support, which is an important step. Perhaps Viola is beginning to grow into her new role as a music therapist.

The final episode of Viola's story takes place about one year after she first began work, when she attends a support group. Let's meet her there...

In which Viola attends a meeting

Viola opened the door and went in.

She was greeted by a sea of unfamiliar faces sitting around a large round table, on which an enticing buffet lunch was set out. Viola sat down at a vacant seat, muttered 'hello', and looked around the room feeling rather shy and new again. She had come to her first support group meeting, which was for all music therapists working in children's hospices. There seemed to be around 12 faces, of varying ages, mostly women, a couple of men as well. The faces looked friendly, but Viola didn't know any of them apart from Gloria, who was sitting opposite her. Gloria waved 'hello' and continued with her conversation. Viola caught herself looking for badges, didn't see any, and decided that perhaps this didn't matter.

After eating the rather delicious lunch, everyone was invited to give an update on how their work was going in their particular hospice. Viola didn't have much to say, as she still felt rather new, but was interested to hear about everyone else's work. People seemed able to talk honestly, so as well as hearing about new developments, such as work with siblings and the use of music technology, there was talk of frustrations with other members of staff, lack of time and so on. All too soon it was time to set the next meeting date, and also plan to make time for improvising at the next meeting.

There was a lot to think about as Viola drove home.

★

Viola has come a long way since we first encountered her. To begin with, she felt uncertain in many ways, unsure of her role, and so hung up about her particular theoretical perspective that it was difficult for her to know how to begin. However, she has found help and support from Gloria and from her other colleagues and this has helped her to become more confident in her new role. As she becomes a member of this group, consisting of other music therapists, she again feels new and rather shy, but now her shyness is accompanied by a new feeling of growing self-confidence.

Viola still clings to some of her old habits, such as wondering about which training course the other therapists have done.

I hope that you, as reader, feel that Viola will continue to be open to the possibility of change and personal development, that she will receive the support which others are able to offer and that she will also be able to support others in their journey towards becoming a therapist.

Coda

On a personal note, I wrote this chapter in the style of a children's story as a way of exploring some personal experiences in a way that was not too heavy or discouraging. I showed early drafts to colleagues at the hospice where I work, and was pleasantly surprised by their comments. I was moved when our Head of Care said that she had cried as she read the part about saying good-bye to Peter. I am less confident about how other music therapists may react, but hope that there will be something in this chapter to which they can relate. When a music therapist begins working in a children's hospice, it is a bit like entering another world. My motto in the very early days was, 'Everything's different here – different rules apply!' This thought kept me going as I began the difficult process of adapting music therapy to a hospice environment – rewriting the 'rules' if you like. I was given a lot of support and encouragement from other music therapists who work in children's hospices, and also by Lesley Schatzberger, who is the force behind Jessie's Fund. I hope that anyone considering hospice work will be encouraged by the stories in this book. Finally, I would like to pay tribute to the many children and families living with life-threatening conditions with whom I have made music; their lives are the inspiration for this chapter.

Before we conclude...

The narratives in this book have presented music therapy through the minds of dedicated professionals. What about the 'other side' of these music therapy stories? What about the children, the young folk, those who are ill, distraught, afraid, uncomfortable, confused – how does music therapy seem to them?

It seems fitting to conclude this book with 19-year-old Chris Stratton speaking of his experiences of life, music, illness, school and music therapy with Jane Mayhew.

Mercédès Pavlicevic

Chris describing his musical ideas to Jane. Photo: Jim Four

Conclusion: Working together in music therapy

Chris Stratton and Jane Mayhew

Jane

Chris is 19 years old and has been coming to Demelza House for music therapy sessions for over five years. He lives close to the hospice and is able to come for regular individual sessions, which last for about an hour. He has a great love for a wide variety of musical genres and particularly seems to enjoy writing his own songs.

Chris has Leigh's disease, a condition he says he 'knows very little about'. His description is very graphic. 'It's like an epileptic person experiencing a seizure, but I'm awake, I can think.' The condition 'changes a hell of a lot and I can have sudden seizures in my legs, arms and neck'. His seizures can last for minutes or for several hours. It's essential for him to rest his body and save energy, and if he doesn't get a good sleep, the next day can be affected. He says that for years he was trying to find out about the disease to discover what was wrong with him. He is annoyed that his condition is degenerative and that his is the only adult form on record. 'Some have lived on, but most die when they are children, unable to do anything for themselves.'

He was originally diagnosed with 'muscle migraines' and, when he was three years old, Leigh's disease was confirmed. As a toddler he always walked with a limp and his parents took him to doctors. 'I haven't accepted it – but I'm past caring about getting rid of it. I've lived with it for so long. If it gets taken away from me I'll be able to do all the stuff I haven't ever done. But if I didn't have it [Leigh's] I wouldn't have done all the things I've done.'

After primary school he spent two years at mainstream secondary school, before receiving hospital school education. Secondary school was not what he had hoped for: it was not accessible with a wheelchair, there were no lifts and few ramps. In 1998 Chris stayed at the hospice for two weeks. His immune system 'went on the blink' and he could barely see, hear, speak or move. He was 14, and was admitted on New Year's Eve. I got to know Chris after this stay at Demelza.

Chris

I actually find it quite strange writing about 'myself', questioning my own senses and so on…in fact I find 'me'…as a case to study, highly boring, and if I were a college course I bet the students would be asleep before they even began research, and thus…not pass. That is the original reason I began writing in the first place.

I recall hearing 'I'd Do Anything For Love (But I Won't Do That)' by Meat Loaf on the radio and watching it played constantly on the Saturday chart show on television when I was about nine, and thinking, 'Yes! I've never heard (or seen) anything like this before.' I received the album that Easter from my Gran, and discovered that the majority of each song lasts over seven minutes. Each track is so cinematic in its own right, which got me interested in film-making. Of course, a good film is always accompanied by a half-decent soundtrack. I began rummaging through my parents' CD/LP and cassette collection and recording various tracks I felt were relevant to the idea of the film I had in mind (mostly involving monsters, aliens, ghosts, robots etc.).

Then I thought, 'Well…films I am watching – e.g. *Ghostbusters* and *E.T.* – have an interesting blend of popular music and also contain eeriness and atmospherics, ambient/"emotion" music.' So I began listening to rather obscure groups, such as Enigma, and Peter Gabriel and Roxy Music, and not forgetting David Bowie, and thus gaining inspiration to give a stab at writing my own material.

The result was inspired by [Meat Loaf's] *Bat Out Of Hell* and existed purely as lyrics on paper (which later became poetry), which gave more inspiration for my film project. Anyway, as time went on, the unknown lyrics (which I refer to as 'Like A Human Vampire') got lost, and because I didn't write music or invent a melody for them, haven't been rediscovered.

★

I remember the transition from primary to secondary school education and it symbolising (for me personally) the point where we take our metamorphosis from childhood into a whole new realm, a virgin territory which has never experienced your footprint and where you are expected to conform to an entirely alien concept and whole new way of life. Having been an avid viewer of *Grange Hill* for some months and having heard of my Uncle Paul's exploits and recollections of his 'days as a "lad"' and so forth, I had done my own research and thought I was prepared for the next step, but…as usual…how wrong was I?

★

My Uncle Paul has also opened my wide and varied tastes in music, films and life in general. In fact if you ask me…he actually helped me to enjoy what little childhood and 'fun' I was able to experience. My family have all commented on their own contribution to making my life as 'enjoyable as possible' but I would actually class my Uncle Paul as my best friend when I was growing up. He was one of the few people (family members) around whom I felt I could be myself and speak my mind and voice my opinions, plus it helps that we have a mutual agreement on subjects we feel strongly about (politics, the modern way things are heading, philosophical situations, the television and music etc.). It was right from when I used to visit Gran and Uncle Paul on Saturdays and occasionally on weekdays that he exposed me to The Trogs, The Kinks, Deep Purple, The Who etc., and used to show me his comics and watch television with me (especially *The Incredible Hulk* and later on Steven King's *It*). He also used to take me to the woods and fields and construct bows and arrows, we used to collect conkers, not to fight with, to admire and say, 'Yes…look at what I found, and I had a bloody good time doing it too.' Plus we've always had an fascination with the unexplained and paranormal occurrences and so on, so we used to just sit and have a chat that would then alter into a monologue each. Then the conversation would take a total left turn and we'd find ourselves waffling on about something completely unrelated but quite relevant on our part anyway.

To this day we still get on like a house on fire but instead of playing around like children, we continue yapping like two old men with itches in areas they can't reach in public places.

I found secondary school quite strange at first. I was used to being the youngest in my class, at the local county primary school, until I chose to stay on an extra year because I wanted more of a chance to know my schoolmates. I was suddenly surrounded by students younger than I, and whom I didn't know, making me feel like an 'alien'. This, I found later, I could use to my advantage, and would humour myself by playing 'mind-games' with the pupils, staff and visitors who had a shred of ignorance about them, e.g. someone would see me in my chair struggling > then walk away > next, they'd go watch a game of Rounders and who'd be running round the field... Yours truly!

By December 1996, everyone had, to an extent, settled down and got used to the school grounds, friendships had formed, I was a fairly popular, charismatic, humorous personality who got on with almost everyone (my tutor group surely warmed to me) and Christmas was just around the corner.

★

Then I hit 13 and I started to discover just how much of a dramatic change was occurring. I felt that school was holding me back; I wanted to move along and to be included, not given 'special treatment'. I didn't want any help in getting along. As far as I was concerned the whole world was against me... I was within inches of a detonator but these mutant serpent-like creatures with wide pulsating white eyes with blue, black and red coloured veins holding me back...with their arms...eight fingers, and two thumbs. However, that would be a lot stranger, because amphibians don't have five digits on each hand. They haven't even got hands, nor do they have arms…

This little episodic farce became a trigger of inspiration…and from then on I classed myself as…a Rebel. (Quick definition – 'Rebel > A person who rebels. To fight against or refuse allegiance to an established government or conversations; realist > to take control of.')

As I saw things, I was young, highly determined and yearned for as much control as I could handle. Looking back on this period: on one hand the word 'selfish' comes to mind, but on the other hand… Isn't that what everyone wants at the end of the day?

I began writing sentences as a kind of 'self-therapy' to deal with the depression I was going through. When I started out making phrases on the inner coverings of my tutor-books to pass the time and…boredom. Even in break time instead of getting involved with a deep conversation debating 'which Spice Girl do you fancy most?' etc., I would go and find a quiet area and just sit under a tree (for example). I would overhear or observe my mates talking to each other and, while absorbing the all-round scenery, began 'slicing and dicing' the language and mannerisms. From that – managed to create a sort of 'sushi concoction' of all sorts, including the music I was listening to that day, a film I had just seen, a book I had read, a lesson that I had found 'interesting', my mates, my home life and…me.

After two years in mainstream secondary education I was starting to feel like a complete 'whale out of the ocean' (more so than I already knew). Plus, to say that the maximum amount of hours that I received for 'special support' was unfair is a complete understatement. To top things off, I was under the impression that the school was getting annoyed at the amount of time I was spending at home due to my ill health, which led to my further depression. Anyway, this only made my lyrics and music more dark and introspective (full of curse-words, references to sexual perversion, death 'n destruction, etc.). I mean, I've had my certain fascination with the process of life and death and the obscure for as long as I can remember. (Stemming back from the times spent with Uncle Paul giving me my cynical views on things – which is both a good thing and a bad thing – good because I am able to question things and create my own individual judgement, and bad because I do it all the time. It's okay to be a cynical person, but when you are an overall 'cynic', that's taking things a wee bit too far, in my opinion, which adds to my personality.) I wasn't happy where I was at the time and I'd wander around the complex of the school, on my own.

★

From numerous conversations with my mum and dad, we decided it wasn't worth me being in that place since they weren't giving me the support I obviously needed and was entitled to. So I pulled out and was out of school for six months plus. The more my illness was becoming unsustainable, the more down and depressed and…bored I got.

Mum later got in touch with Jackie Locke from the West Kent Hospital School for home tuition. However, when she visited, had a chat with Mum and then a chat with me, Jackie finally said to Mum, 'He doesn't need home schooling, he needs to be in school.' So from then onwards things were looking on the up…

I began West Kent (later 'Woodview Campus') in the beginning of 1998 and still felt like an outcast. I had been made aware beforehand that the school is specifically for those integrating from 'special' to 'main-stream', pupils who are out of educating and those with, for instance, ADHD. Although I noticed the reason I was there, I still thought no one was on my wave length.

Anyway the rest of the school year wasn't the most optimistic time for me, personally. However, among the tutors, who were all fantastic at what they did, I found that my English teacher, Mrs Williams, was the one with whom I struck a bond and she encouraged me to write more. But I wasn't getting the respect of the pupils. I felt left out most of the break, and any social time, and even at the very beginning I experienced minor bullying, which at least helped me to write stronger songs.

That summer, I met up with some old friends that I had known since primary school and we would practise with the guitar and vocals and decided to form a band. We had no drummer until one day I thought about having a 'bash' on the drums in my garage and my friend on the guitar – I don't think we had a name, but it was one of the most active summers I've had.

Then after the holidays ended, I still kept in touch with my friends but the band idea dissolved...they lost complete interest and we decided to call it a day; besides,

1.   we couldn't play our instruments very well and

2.   we were crap.

As for school, it was the same up, constant taunts from the pupils, loads of support from the teachers, but when the Christmas holidays came around, my life and songwriting drastically altered for the better and the worse.

In the early December of 1998 I caught a cold. Because my immune system is all 'topsy-turvy' I would get tired easily and would sleep during the day. At times I would stare at my hands and think, 'Am I growing old because some celestial force is sucking my life force like the moon to the tide?' Gradually I got more ill and was admitted into Demelza House Children's Hospice on New Year's Eve and spent about two or three weeks there.

I have used the music room at Demelza House as long as I've been attending, and I've known Jane the same amount of time. It wasn't until I was completely better that I actually began seeing Jane for music sessions. The term 'music therapy' is kind of the wrong title for our meetings, although the music we make turns around to equal a question which Jane asks me, and it's more like having jamming routines: musicians gathering together not knowing what to expect to achieve.

Jane and I have a good conversationalist relationship and I've worked some things out – that's the reason I can get the styles of music that I see in my vision out through her. When I've worked with friends attempting to produce an *avant garde* 'masterpiece', it has always turned out dissolving because although they may understand my lyrics (which are weird, twisted and deep), unless you understand me mentally the music won't get completed. Jane and I share the same sense of humour which helps because on my first session I brought my electric guitar and we sang a song I wrote called 'Strangers When We Meet'. As soon as I translated (vocally) the chord structure, she immediately understood the rest of the rhythm which is complex. I've even brought a friend who was in my original group over for a session but he didn't want to continue.

We also have a bloody good 'laugh'. We understand one another. When I say 'grey', normally someone assumes either 'black' or 'white'; not Jane, she…thinks 'grey'.

Since then, I've been to college where I've experienced emotional highs and lows, and illness and time off, stress and fights and fall-outs. I've written songs based on those situations. Along with joining a youth club and forging new friendships, which also help me write. But then again I've also lost friends in the lifeline since, which has led to songs about isolation and alienation, and of course the exploration of space travel and wonder.

Chris the Rebel

Jessie's Fund CD track

7. 'Grounded' – Chris Stratton

List of contributors

Gill Cubitt

Gill Cubitt studied music at Reading University, where she also trained as a teacher. After teaching music for many years within mainstream schools, Gill retrained as a music therapist at Roehampton, University of Surrey. Gill began working at East Anglia's Children's Hospices, Quidenham, shortly after qualifying as a music therapist. Gill has also worked privately in Norfolk; her client groups have included bereaved children, autistic children and adults, children with moderate to severe learning difficulties and those with sensory impairment.

Gill has recently completed her MA in music therapy, which looked at some of the differences and challenges experienced by music therapists working in children's hospices in the UK. When time allows, Gill continues to enjoy teaching and playing the violin, and playing piano in a swing band.

Graeme Davis

Initially having trained as a professional musician, Graeme Davis studied music therapy at the Nordoff–Robbins Music Therapy Centre in London. Currently he works full time as a music therapist at the Pasque Hospice, near Luton.

Neil Eaves

Neil Eaves works at Rainbows Children's Hospice in Loughborough, which cares for children living in the East Midlands and South Yorkshire. He also works within special schools and has worked in a variety of other settings previously. He studied music at the University of Newcastle upon Tyne, where he specialised in studio recording, which is now a big hobby of his when he gets (any) spare time. Neil would like to thank all of those involved in the production of this book who helped to transform his waffle into something that is (he hopes) coherent and useful.

Elinor Everitt

Elinor Everitt graduated with a music degree, specialising in piano accompaniment, from Royal Holloway College, University of London, in 1996. She then worked for a year in a home for adults with severe learning disabilities and for two years in a residential school for children with profound and multiple learning disabilities. In 2000 Elinor qualified as a music therapist at Anglia Polytechnic University. She works in a special needs school with children aged four to 19, who have a range of learning and physical disabilities, including autism. She was also a part of the outreach music therapy team at the local children's hospice, and gained her MA in 2004 writing about this innovative work.

Cathy Ibberson

Cathy Ibberson began further education by training as a registered general nurse (RGN) at St James's University Hospital in Leeds from 1981 to 1984. After working in care of the elderly for a year she spent a 'year out' travelling in Israel and the United States. She then went on to specialise in working with children and gained her registered children's nurse (RSCN) qualification in 1987.

Following two years working in children's orthopaedics and general surgery within the National Health Service Cathy then turned to palliative care, working on the multidisciplinary team at Martin House Children's Hospice for a year. Cathy then went on to study for a BA music degree at Bretton Hall College, Wakefield, following which she studied music therapy at Roehampton Institute. She qualified as a music therapist in 1994. Since then she has worked primarily as a part-time music therapist at Martin House while raising a young family.

Jane Mayhew

Jane Mayhew has been working at Demelza House Children's Hospice since 1999. Her role at the hospice includes running individual and group sessions for children, young people and their families. She also offers individual and group sessions for bereaved children and runs a music specialist training programme for staff. Jane has also worked with adults with learning disabilities and children who have emotional and behavioural problems. Jane qualified as a music therapist in 1998 following her masters degree in music from the University of York. She studied music therapy at Anglia Polytechnic University, Cambridge, and gained her Masters in music therapy in 2003. She has also presented work both nationally (World Congress for Music Therapy) and internationally (European Music Therapy Congress). In 2003 Jane worked in a children's institution in Northern Romania with the charity Music as Therapy, setting up a music programme for the children and training Romanian staff.

Kathryn Nall

Kathryn Nall graduated from Manchester University in 1974 with an honours degree in economic and social studies, having specialised in social administration. After experience in both residential and field social work she gained a diploma in social work (CQSW) at Exeter University in 1976. As a social worker Kathryn worked in a variety of settings within both local authorities and the voluntary sector. This included work as a social worker at an inner London hospital and later developing an early counselling service for parents of children newly diagnosed with a severe learning difficulty. Kathryn has also co-ordinated a large respite care scheme for adults with a learning disability. While continuing to work as a social worker, Kathryn followed a serious interest in music, which led to an LGSM (singing) in 1985 and some teaching. She continued musical studies in piano and violin, and then trained as a music therapist at Anglia Polytechnic University in 1995, gaining an MA in March 2001. Having worked for four years as music therapist at a children's hospice, she now works in schools as part of a team of music therapists within an education service.

Mercédès Pavlicevic

Mercédès Pavlicevic is a graduate of the Nordoff–Robbins Centre, London, and of Edinburgh University. Since 1991 she has lived in South Africa where she is Associate Professor, and Director of the Music Therapy Programme, at the University of Pretoria, South Africa. She has published extensively in the field of music therapy, and is delighted to be a part of this book.

Ceridwen Rees

Ceridwen Rees has been music therapist at Helen House since November 1998. Having graduated from Kingston Polytechnic in 1986, she moved to Oxford where she developed a peripatetic oboe/piano teaching practice. As time went on she became more interested in the responses of her students to the music they were playing, rather than simply in their interpretation of the music. Having benefited from some counselling during this time, Ceridwen combined these two elements and took the postgraduate diploma in music therapy course at Bristol University where she was awarded a pass with commendation.

Ceridwen also works as music therapist at a school for children with special needs, and she is in the process of setting up a charitably funded music therapy post on the children's wards at the John Radcliffe Hospital in Oxford. She has also developed the music at her daughter's former primary school, both as a class music teacher and in establishing a school choir.

From can-crushing and the 1812 Overture in class lessons to giving a nervous child the confidence to sing solo in the school choir, from Christmas carols round the tree at the hospice accompanied by her band 'Horrendous Harmonics!' to singing at a child's funeral service, Ceridwen has experienced how music has the capacity to reach out and accompany people in their hugely diverse journeys through life and into death.

Lesley Schatzberger

A professional clarinet player, Lesley Schatzberger studied at the Royal Manchester College of Music, the University of York and the Royal Academy of Music. She has specialised in performance on historical instruments but at the same time has been active in the field of contemporary music.

She was principal clarinet in Roger Norrington's London Classical Players and now holds that position in John Eliot Gardiner's English Baroque Soloists and Orchestre Révolutionnaire et Romantique. In addition, she has played regularly with the Academy of Ancient Music, with which she has also appeared as concerto soloist. At the other end of the musical spectrum, she toured extensively with Stockhausen's own ensemble. She teaches at the University of York.

In 1994 her younger daughter Jessica died at the age of nine years, six months after the diagnosis of a brain tumour. Jessie's Fund was registered as a UK charity the following year, and since then Lesley has devoted an increasing amount of time to running the charity, with the aim that as many children with special needs as possible can benefit from music therapy and other forms of creative music-making.

Brigitte Schwarting

Brigitte Schwarting grew up in a family of musicians in Freiburg, in southern Germany. She learned piano and violin from an early age and went to music college in Berlin after finishing school. She enrolled for a piano pedagogy course, studied with Professor Klaus Hellwig and graduated in 1988. Then she went to the City University London, Nordoff–Robbins Music Therapy Centre, to train as a music therapist.

Following her diploma she worked at Ravenswood Village, Berkshire, with Senior Music Therapist Sandra Brown for one year, before returning to Berlin to do further study in piano performance with Professor Rolf Koenen and working as a music therapist with adults with learning disabilities. After her diploma in 1992, she married an Englishman and lived in Warwickshire for four years, working as a music therapist for the County Music Service and raising a family, before moving up to Manchester in 1996.

She now works at a hospice as well as a school for autistic children. She helps with a special needs music group and teaches the piano, as well as directing a small choir at the German church in Manchester and holding music sessions for the children at the German Saturday School.

Chris Stratton

My name is Chris Stratton and I am 19 years old (soon to be pushing 20 – eh!). I find the concept of 'the future' personally uncertain and rather intimidating.

I live with my mum, dad, sister (Becky) and our cat (Sadie) in Aylesford, near Maidstone. My mum looks after my cousins Louie and Hannah (my best friends) during the week. I enjoy spending time with them especially because they seem to enjoy my ways of 'humouring' them, and we are fond of different styles of music. I also see family members during the week with Mum, if I feel well.

I have a girlfriend (Nicky) who I don't see that often but love very much. We were introduced by Kim Seal of Toggle (Kent Youth) at Strood Youth Club. I am a great fan of David Bowie and the artists he has influenced. I enjoy films, art, and anything 'weird'. I take time out to stroll around the area I live to gain inspiration for films, songs and stories. I obviously have a passion for varied tastes in music and am looking to pursue that.

Catherine Sweeney-Brown

Catherine Sweeney-Brown was born in Ireland, and studied music at Bangor University, Wales, where she specialised in solo performance, before training as a music therapist at Anglia Polytechnic University, Cambridge. She has worked as a music therapist in children's hospices since 1997, and also works in the fields of acquired brain injury and adult learning disability. She is involved in education within children's hospices and recently had a chapter on her work published in *Psychodynamic Music Therapy: Case Studies*. She teaches both flute and piano, regularly performing in vocal ensembles and orchestras, as well as playing solo flute.

Diane Wilkinson

Diane Wilkinson is an experienced music therapist and qualified teacher from Cardiff. Her music therapy clients span the generations, ranging from small babies to senior citizens. Diane also teaches woodwind instruments and piano to children in Cardiff and the Vale of Glamorgan, having qualified with a BEd (Hons) from the Royal Welsh College of Music and Drama in 1993. She trained as a music therapist under the tuition of Professor Leslie Bunt at the University of Bristol, gaining a postgraduate diploma in music therapy in 1997 and attaining state registration in 1999.

With such a diverse client base, Diane comes into contact with a broad spectrum of conditions and health needs, ranging from children with life-limiting conditions, such as those with whom she works at Tŷ Hafan, the Children's Hospice of Wales, through to people with learning disabilities who are adapting to life in the community. The proud mother of a new baby daughter, Diane lives in Cardiff with her husband.

List of Jessie's Fund CD tracks

Jessie's Fund: 'Music from Children's Hospices'

This CD may be obtained from Jessie's Fund directly, using the order form at the back of this book.

1. 'Bridge over Troubled Water' – Jessica P. (Ceridwen Rees, Helen House – Chapter 5)

2. Main riff – Tom (Neil Eaves, Rainbows – Chapter 6)

3. Solo riff – Tom (Neil Eaves, Rainbows – Chapter 6)

4. 'Everybody Sucks' – Tom (Neil Eaves, Rainbows – Chapter 6)

5. 'Chilled' – Imran (Neil Eaves, Rainbows – Chapter 6)

6. 'Ultimate Bass' – Imran (Neil Eaves, Rainbows – Chapter 6)

7. 'Grounded' – Chris Stratton (Chris Stratton/Jane Mayhew, Demelza House – Conclusion)

Additional tracks

8. 'Evergreen' – Ray (Catherine Sweeney-Brown, Hope House – Chapter 3)

9. 'Running' – Stuart Wickison (Jane Mayhew, Demelza House – Chapter 4)

10. 'Climb Every Mountain' – Yasmin Harris (Catherine Sweeney-Brown, Hope House – Chapter 3)

11. 'My Heart Bleeds' – Brendan (Neil Eaves, Rainbows – Chapter 6)

12. 'Celtic Blessing' (Ceridwen Rees, Helen House – Chapter 5)

13. 'Searching the Skies' – settings by David Blake of poems by Jessica George (Lesley Schatzberger – Chapter 1)

Subject index

Acorns 33–4
adolescence
    experienced by teenagers with MD 98
    see also teenagers
adult patients 131–3, 137
aims, of music therapy 100
alternative treatments 26
audio recordings 91–2, 106, 108, 129

bereaved siblings
    groups 43–5, 62–3, 64–79
    outreach work 155, 158
    see also siblings
bereavement *see* grief; loss
Betty Robinson House 124, 125
    day care 128–9
    IPU 127, 136–7
Bohemian Rhapsody (Queen) 95–6
boundaries
    of music therapy 41, 42
    in sibling bereavement group 66
brain
    musical 59–60
    response to music 50–1
brain tumours, intolerance of frequencies
    53
breaks, in group session timetable 74
breathing pattern, working with 46, 49,
    51–4, 60

cabasa, use of 115, 117
calendar, of sessions timetable 67
case studies
    adult improvisation 131–3
    benefits of singing 52–3
    bereaved siblings groups 44–5
    breathing pattern 46, 51–2, 52–3, 54
    Down's syndrome 129–30
    fear reduction 55
    infants 84–6, 134–5
    micro-response to music 89–90
    music technology with teenage boys
        101–8
    musical relationship 46
    open group sessions 113–23
    outreach services 43, 148–9, 151–2,
        153–4, 155, 156

patients near death 55, 84–6, 89–91,
    137
power of creativity 56–8
relaxation sessions 130–1, 142
challenge, of music therapy in hospices
    45–6
children
    need for 'silly' behaviour 69–70
    response to grief 63–4
    working with 133–4, 136
children's hospices
    Acorns 33–4
    Demelza House 62–3, 64–79, 176–7
    development of music therapy 33–4,
        40
    Francis House 110–23
    Helen House 82, 83–93
    hospice life 29, 139–40
    Keech House 126–7, 128, 129–30,
        131–6
    Martin House 27, 28–31, 37–8, 40–7
    Pasque Hospice 124–38
    Tŷ Hafan 139–46
Christmas celebrations 140–1
clapping 120
cognitive ability, and response to music 50
comatose state 59
communication, in outreach work 150
complementary therapy 26
concert performance, by teenager with MD
    104
creativity, power of 56–8
Cubase SX 102

death
    bringing child's body to hospice
        165–6
    children's perception of 64–5
    discussion by siblings 72, 75
    fear of, use of music 56
    work with dying patients 55, 84–6,
        89–91, 137
Demelza House 62–3, 64–79, 176–7
designated weekends, for older adolescents
    98–9
directed improvisations 68, 70–2
Down's Syndrome 129–30
drums, use of 90, 151, 153, 165

electric guitar
    use of 55, 101–3
    see also guitar; midi-guitar

emotions
    exploration by bereaved siblings 70–1,
        72–3
    expression 77, 78, 100, 107
    of music therapists 84, 86
environment
    for group sessions 112–13
    music therapy room 83, 128
epilepsy 53, 89
equipment, medical, effect on therapy 49
evaluation
    group sessions 79, 121–3
    outreach services 157–8

families
    care by hospices 29, 37–8, 111
    changes following death 72, 77
    involvement in outreach therapy 152
    role of siblings in bereavement 68, 77
    support for bereavement 62
    thanksgiving services for 143–6
    see also siblings
fear reduction 54–6
feelings *see* emotions
F.G. Syndrome 89
film music, interest in writing 171
Fleetingly known, yet ever remembered (poem)
    145
flute, use of 54, 55, 59–60, 142
Francis of Assisi, Saint 111, 144
Francis House 110–23
free improvisation 69, 76–7
fundraising 34–5
funerals
    music for 92–3
    see also remembrance services

Garden of Remembrance 145
George, Jessica *see* Jessie
GIM (Guided Imagery in Music) 50
goodbye, saying (death of child) 165–6
grief 63, 64
    see also loss
group scream 70
groups *see* open group sessions; peer
    support; siblings, groups
Guardian Jerwood Award for Community
    Achievement 35
Guided Imagery in Music (GIM) 50
guilt, of siblings 75
guitar
    use of 45, 52–3, 54, 85, 90, 119–20
    see also electric guitar; midi-guitar

hand chimes, use of 115, 119
happiness, guilt of siblings 75
Helen House 82, 83–93
home life, discussion by siblings 72, 75
home visiting, music therapy 42, 43,
    147–58
hospice life 29, 139–40
humour 126

identity, of bereaved siblings 71, 77–8
improvisations
    in group work 67–9, 70–2, 73–4,
        76–7
    work with adults 131–3
induction, of new music therapists 163–4
infants
    mother/infant model of relationships
        45–6
    near death 84–6
    work with 134–5
instruments
    exploration in group 66
    to represent family 71
    used in therapy 65
    see also names of individual instruments;
        percussion instruments

Jessie
    personality 22–3
    illness
        development 23–5
        treatment 26
        remission 26–8
        deterioration 28–30
    poems 21, 27
    death 30
Jessie's Fund 18
    charitable status 31
    focus following Jessie's death 30
    original purpose 27
    stimulating greater use of music
        therapists 35–6
    supporting music therapy in hospices
        32–5
    Victoria Wood as patron 35
job-share 42–3

Keech House 126–7, 128, 129–30,
    131–6
keyboard
    use of 105, 106
    see also piano

Leigh's disease 170–1
loss
    of expectations for child 151
    feelings of siblings 76, 79
    see also grief
lyre, use of 54

Make me a channel of your peace (poem) 144
Martin House 37–8, 40–7
    Jessie's stay 27, 28–31
MD (muscular dystrophy) 96–7
medical condition, effect on therapy 48–9
medical equipment, effect on therapy 49
micro-responses 59–60
midi-guitar
    use of 55
    see also electric guitar; guitar
midicreator technology 59, 60
mother/infant model, for client
    relationships 45–6
muscular dystrophy (MD) 96–7
music
    enabling expression of feelings 136
    in hospice life 139–40, 146
    physiological effects 50
    power to energize 15–16, 56–8, 81–2
    value of 137–8
music technology
    advantages for disabled performers 96
    enabling realization of dreams 108
    use with teenagers 102–3
music therapists
    career paths 38–40, 82, 178–81
    peer group support 34, 150, 164, 167
    role 16, 41–2, 111
    story of first experiences 161–8
    vulnerability 17
music therapy
    benefits 151, 157–8
    challenge of hospices 45–6
    development in children's hospices
        31–2, 33–4, 40, 147–8
    introducing children to 99–100, 165
    value of 87, 93, 121
Music Therapy Home Visiting Service
    147–58
musical brain 59–60
    see also brain
musical relationships 46
    patient's view 176–7
musicogenic epilepsy 53

'naming an emotion' improvisation 70–1
network meetings
    hospice music therapists 34
    see also peer support
normality, for siblings in music therapy 88

oboe, use of 90
open group sessions 111–23
outreach services 42, 147–58

pain management, through music therapy
    49–51
parents, positive interaction with child
    151
Pasque Hospice 124–38
passive listening 131
patients, personal perspective 171–7
'peace-lovers and warriors' improvisation
    78
peer support, for music therapists 34, 150,
    164, 167
penny whistle, use of 44
percussion instruments 44, 54, 57, 71,
    115, 163
performance, of music at concert 104
persistent vegetative states 59–60
personal perspective, of patient 171–7
physical condition, effect on music therapy
    48–9
physiological effects, of music 50
piano
    use of 44, 51–2, 54, 118
    see also keyboard
planning sessions 114–15
professional issues, in outreach work 150

'quiet rooms' 106

recordings
    audio 91–2, 106, 108
    video 126
reduced states of consciousness 59–60
referential improvisation 71
relationship, with patients 45–6, 176–7
relaxation, using breathing patterns 51–2
relaxation sessions 130–1, 142–3
remembrance services 143–6
    see also funerals
respiration *see* breathing pattern

response to music
  and cognition 50
  emotional release 92–3, 136
  in reduced state of consciousness
    59–60
role, of music therapists 16, 41–2, 111
role play, of teenagers in music therapy
  105, 107

saxophone, use of 43
saying goodbye (death of child) 165–6
school transition 172
schools
  experiences of patient 172, 173,
    174–6
  outreach music therapy 43, 156
screaming
  from distress, effect of music therapy
    51
  group scream 70
sessions
  bereaved siblings group 65–79
  effect of break in timetable 74
  creativity with patients dying 83
  form 42–3, 65
  with teenagers with MD 99–100
  see also open group sessions
siblings
  role in bereaved family 68, 77
  feelings of guilt 75
  groups 43–5, 62–3, 64–79
  involvement in patient sessions
    119–20
  outreach work with 152–4, 155, 158
  recording song for funeral 91–2
  support at hospices 29, 87–8
  see also families
'silly' behaviour, need for, in bereaved
  children 69–70
singing 54, 85–6, 90–1, 115–16, 149,
  151–2
  for breathing control 52–3
  see also vocalisation
songs, providing memory of brother who
  died 92–3
structured approach, of sessions 134
suffering, explored in group sessions 76
supervision, of music therapists 42
support, for music therapists 34, 150, 164,
  167

tactile approach 151
tambour, use of 67
tambourine, use of 43, 117
teamwork 41
teenage units 38
teenagers
  designated weekends 98
  receptiveness to idea of music therapy
    99–100
  response to popular music 95
  special unit 38
  see also adolescence
thanksgiving services 143–6
  see also funerals
touch, use of 151
training
  in medical procedures 49
  for music therapy in hospices 32–3,
    162
Tŷ Hafan 139–46

value, of music therapy 87, 93, 121
verbal expression, and music 71–2, 104
video recording 126
vocalisation 51, 142, 149, 153, 156, 163
  screaming 70
  see also singing

wheelchairs, of teenagers with MD 107
wind-chimes, use of 86, 134, 135
Wood, Victoria 11–13, 35

xylophone, use of 44

Author index

Aagard, T. 122
Aldridge, D. 56

Bailey, L.M. 50
Bean, J. 67
Bick, E. 45–6
Bion, W. 69
Bonny, H.L. 50
Bowlby, J. 63–4
British United Provident Association 50
Bruscia, K. 69, 72–3
Bunt, L. 32, 50
BUPA 50
Burke, K. 70

Colwell, C.M. 50

Dominica, F. 144

Edwards, J. 65
Ende, M. 121

Formisando, R. 59
Foulkes, S.H. 76
Francis of Assisi, Saint 144
Fristad, M.A. 64
Fukuda, Y. 52

Gerberg, K. 97
Grogan, K. 76

Hartley, N. 83
Hemmings, P. 67

Ibberson, C. 65, 104

Klein, J. 45
Knak, D. 76

Miller, C. 50
Muscular Dystrophy Australia 97

Oldfield, A. 67

Parkes, C.M. 64
Pavlicevic, M. 50, 83
Pazola, K.J. 97
Pennells, M. 63
Plach, T. 71
The Power of Music 51

Riviera Smith, C. 95
Rossetti, C. 145

Shaller, J. 95
Smith, S.C. 63
Sood, B. 64
Sutton, J. 158

Towse, E. 72

Weller, E.B. 64
Winnicot, D. 45

Zimmerman, L. 50

Accompanying CD

Music from Children's Hospices is a CD of pieces by young people in hospices around the UK. Some of the songs are referred to in the text of this book. All have been created with the encouragement and guidance of the music therapists whose words you have read in these pages. The young performers are justly proud of their achievement and this CD will move and inspire you.

An added bonus is the inclusion of *Searching the Skies* for children's choir and strings – settings by David Blake of poems by Jessica George. The CD is not for sale commercially, but is available to readers of this book: a donation to Jessie's Fund to cover our costs is warmly invited. £8 per CD is suggested. Please use the order form below.

Please send me .... copies of *Music from Children's Hospices* CD.

Donations accepted by cheque or postal order in UK sterling only (payable to **Jessie's Fund**). Credit card donations can also be accepted in sterling, euros or US dollars, via our website: www.jessiesfund.org.uk. Simply click on the pink 'donate online' button at the bottom of the web page.

☐ I enclose a donation of .... to Jessie's Fund.

☐ I have made a credit card donation of ....via the website

Name..

Address...

....

....Post/Zip Code..........................

Email... Phone ....

If you are a UK taxpayer we can claim back tax you have paid on your donation, making it worth 28% more to us.

☐ I am a UK taxpayer and would like you to claim back tax on my donation.

Please post this form to:

Jessie's Fund, 10 Bootham Terrace, York YO30 7DH, UK

Tel: + 44 (0)1904 658189   Email: info@jessiesfund.org.uk